TREASURY OF LITERATURE

PRACTICE BOOK

WHISPER A SONG
JUMP RIGHT IN
COLOR THE SKY

HARCOURT BRACE & COMPANY

Orlando Atlanta Austin Boston San Francisco Chicago Dallas New York
Toronto London

C O N T E N T S

Printed in the United States of America

ISBN 0-15-301288-9

4 5 6 7 8 9 10   030   97   96   95

WHISPER A SONG

Name _____

Think about the story. Circle each picture that shows an animal the boy says he is like.

bear

lark

lion

toad

fox

poodle

cricket

hen

pig

kitten

whale

tiger

chimp

👉 Read the directions to children. Guide them through the page or have them finish it independently.

Name _____

Read each sentence and the words below it. Write the best word on the line.

1. I see a _____ and a fox.

    will   lion

2. Is the lion _____ ?

    happy   put

3. No, the lion is _____ .

    what   hot

4. Is the _____ happy?

    all   fox

No, the fox is hot!

☞ Read the directions to children. Guide them through the pages or have them finish independently.

GO ON

Name _____

Do you see what I have?

_____

5. I put it _____ on the lion.
           all   and

_____

6. I _____ it all on the fox.
   not   put

_____

7. I put it all on _____.
          no   me

Name _____

A **sentence** is a group of words. It tells a complete idea.
A sentence begins with a capital letter.

Underline the groups of words that are sentences.

1. You have a lion.
have a lion.

2. see the lion.
We see the lion.

3. have a fox.
I have a fox.

4. A lion is not a fox.
is not a fox.

 Read the directions to children. Guide them through the page or
have them finish it independently.

Name _____

Read each sentence and the words below it. Look at each picture. Write the word that best completes each sentence.

_____

1. The fox is on a _____.
   cot   not

_____

2. The fox is _____.
   hot   top

_____

3. The fox is _____ happy.
   pop   not

_____

4. The fox is in a _____.
   pot   top

_____

5. _____ can see the fox.
   Don   Box

Read the directions to children. Guide them through the page or have them finish it independently.

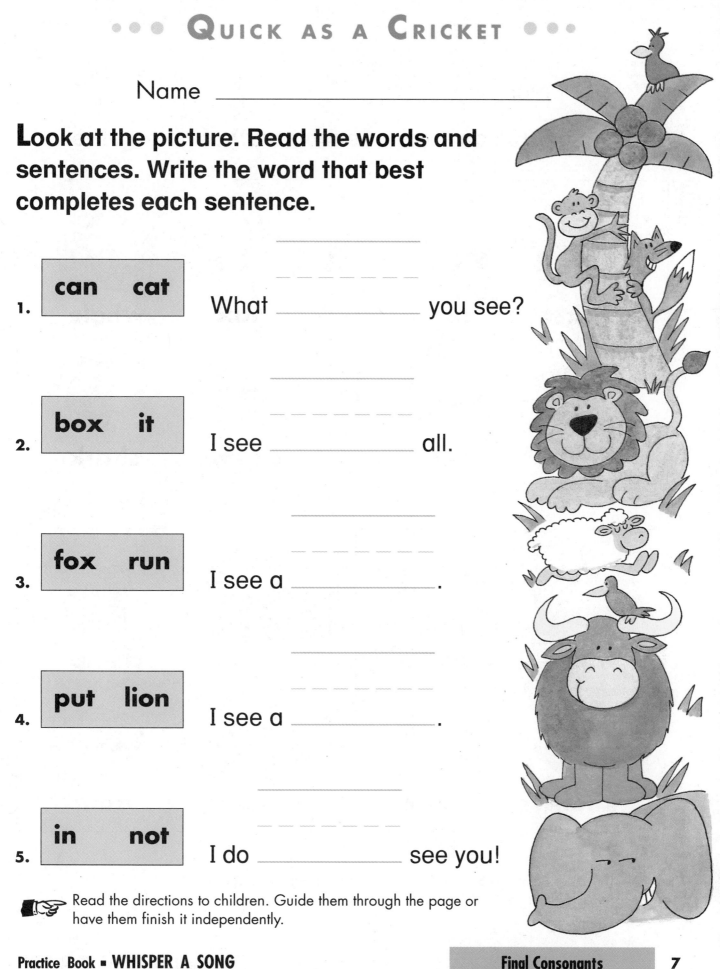

QUICK AS A CRICKET

Name _____

Look at the picture. Read the words and sentences. Write the word that best completes each sentence.

1. | **can   cat** |

What _____ you see?

2. | **box   it** |

I see _____ all.

3. | **fox   run** |

I see a _____.

4. | **put   lion** |

I see a _____.

5. | **in   not** |

I do _____ see you!

Read the directions to children. Guide them through the page or have them finish it independently.

Practice Book ▪ WHISPER A SONG

Final Consonants
/t/t, /ks/x, /n/n

7

HBJ material copyrighted under notice appearing earlier in this work.

Name _____

Circle the three animals in each box that go together.

1.

cricket   ant

lamb   bee

2.

fox   whale

shrimp   shark

3.

whale   poodle

kitten   basset

4.

lion   chimp

tiger   clam

 Read the directions to children. Guide them through the page or have them finish it independently.

Name _____

Circle each picture that shows something the girl in the story learned from a friend.

walk   **kick**   **nap**

cry   **jump**

sing   **throw**   **fly**

run   **read**   **love**

☞ Read the directions to children. Guide them through the page or have them finish it independently.

Name _____

Read each sentence and the words below it.
Write the best word on the line.

_____

1. I'm a _____.

    cat   can

_____

2. I'm a _____.

    hot   horse

_____

3. Do you play _____ all?

    a   at

_____

4. Yes, Horse. You and I can _____.

    play   put

Read the directions to children. Guide them through the pages
or have them finish independently.

GO ON

Name _____

5. I can _____.

       walk   what

6. I can run and _____.

       nap   jump

7. Come on, _____ cat.

       my   I'm

8. You can be a _____.

       happy   friend

Name_____

Words in a sentence are in order.
The words must be in order to make sense.

Write each sentence in order.

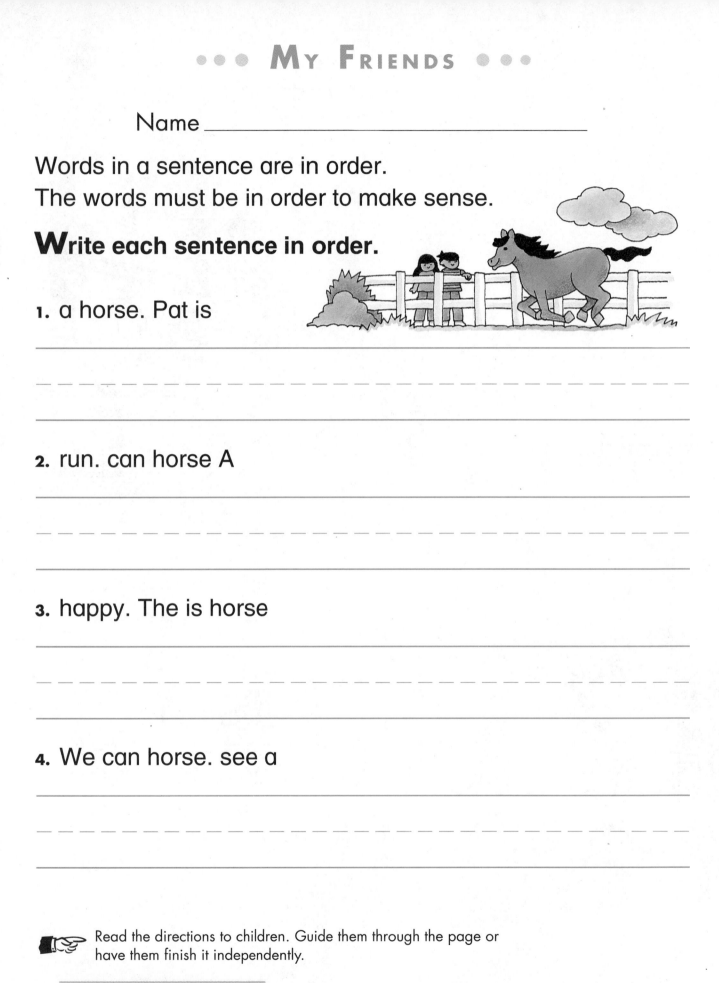

1. a horse. Pat is

_____

- - - - - - - - - - - - - - - - - - - -

_____

2. run. can horse A

- - - - - - - - - - - - - - - - - - - -

_____

3. happy. The is horse

_____

- - - - - - - - - - - - - - - - - - - -

_____

4. We can horse. see a

_____

- - - - - - - - - - - - - - - - - - - -

_____

☞ Read the directions to children. Guide them through the page or
have them finish it independently.

Name _____

Look at the picture. Read each sentence and the words below it. Write the word that best completes each sentence.

1. Do you see the _____?

    cat   cats

2. All the cats can _____.

    play   plays

3. The cat runs and _____.

    jump   jumps

4. Can you see the _____?

    cat   cats

5. The cats do not _____ you.

    see   sees

☞ Read the directions to children. Guide them through the page or have them finish it independently.

Name _____

Read the sentence. Write the letter <u>a</u> to complete each word. Draw a line to the picture that the sentence goes with.

___
___

1. Tab is on a h_____t.

___
___

2. Sox will n_____p.

___
___

3. Dot runs to the m_____n.

___
___

4. Pat is not happy _____t all.

___
___

5. Tan is a happy c_____t.

☞ Read the directions to children. Guide them through the page or have them finish it independently.

Name _____

Read the words in the box. Then read each sentence. Write the word that best completes each sentence.

| tag | can | had | bag | ran |

1. What _____ you play?

2. Can you play _____?

3. I _____ the bag for cans.

4. My cat _____ to see what I did.

5. My cat is in the _____.

 Read the directions to children. Guide them through the page or have them finish it independently.

Name _____

Circle three pictures in each box that go together.

1.
book   desk

crocodile   crayons

2.
owl   bird

ant   hen

3.
computer   apple

banana   orange

4.
game   jacks

sofa   ball

Read the directions to children. Guide them through the page or have them finish it independently.

Name _____

Think about the story. Circle each picture that shows someone Neddy Buttercup woke up.

sheep

lion

pig

fox

horse

dog

cat

👉 Read the directions to children. Guide them through the page or have them finish it independently.

Name _____

Read the sentence and the words below it. Write the word that best completes each sentence.

_____

1. The cat and the _____ can not see.

    do   dog

_____

2. Jump _____ on me!

    up   put

_____

3. The dog got up on the _____.

    pig   in

_____

4. The cat got up _____ the dog.

    no   on

☞ Read the directions to children. Guide them through the pages or have them finish independently.

GO ON ➡

Name _____

_____
- - - - - - - - - - - - - - - - - -

5. Pig! No! Do not go _____!

walking   what

_____
- - - - - - - - - - - - - - - - - -

6. _____ went the cat.

Down   Did

_____
- - - - - - - - - - - - - - - - - -

7. Down _____ the dog.

you   went

_____
- - - - - - - - - - - - - - - - - -

8. The dog and the cat _____ up and down.

got   at

Name _____

A **telling sentence** tells about something or someone. It begins with a capital letter. It ends with a period (.).

Write each sentence correctly.

1. a dog can run

_____

- - - - - - - - - - - - - - - - - - -

_____

2. it can jump

_____

- - - - - - - - - - - - - - - - - - -

_____

3. you walk to me

_____

- - - - - - - - - - - - - - - - - - -

_____

4. cats can play

_____

- - - - - - - - - - - - - - - - - - -

_____

☞ Read the directions to children. Guide them through the page or have them finish it independently.

Name _____

Read the sentences and look at the pictures in each box. Write a word with <u>–ing</u> to tell what is happening.

1.

She can **jump**.

_____

She is _____ .

2.

He will **walk**.

_____

He is _____ .

3.

She can **play**.

_____

She is _____ .

☞ Read the directions to children. Guide them through the page or have them finish it independently.

Name _____

Look at each picture. Read the sentence and the words below it. Write the word that best completes each sentence.

1. Dad got a _____.

                      hat   has

2. I put it _____.

        nod   on

3. The hat went _____!

               fog   in

4. The _____ did it!

    dog   did

Read the directions to children. Guide them through the page or have them finish it independently.

Name _____

Read each sentence and the words below it. Write the word that best completes each sentence.

_____

1. Can you _____ to see me?

       come   comes

_____

2. You can _____ my horse.

      see   sees

_____

3. You can see my _____ nap.

      pig   pigs

_____

4. My dog _____.

      run   runs

_____

5. My _____ play.

      cat   cats

👉 Read the directions to children. Guide them through the page or have them finish it independently.

Name _____

Look at the picture. Read the sentence and the words below it. Write the word that best completes each sentence.

1. The _____ is on the man.

   hot   hat

2. A pig is not a _____.

   dog   got

3. The man got _____.

   mad   ran

4. Can a _____ run?

   fan   at

☞ Read the directions to children. Guide them through the page or have them finish it independently.

Name _____

Look at the picture. Read the words in the box and the sentence. Write the word that tells what will happen.

nap	run

1. Pig will _____ .

walk	jump

2. Pig will _____ .

up	down

3. Pig will go _____ .

☞ Read the directions to children. Guide them through the page or have them finish it independently.

Name _____

Read the sentence and the words below it. Write the word that best completes each sentence.

_____

1. I'm walking, and I see _____.

   brown   from

_____

_____

2. Is it a _____?

   come   cow

_____

_____

3. I see _____.

   and   red

_____

_____

4. Is it the red _____ a fox? What is it?

   of   you

☞ Read the directions to children. Guide them through the pages or have them finish independently.

GO ON

Name _____

5. I see _____ .

got   green

6. I see a _____ of green.

hot   lot

7. It is a _____ !

duck   did

8. I _____ it! Did you?

saw   she

Name _____

Think about the animals the boy saw in the story. Draw a line to show how the boy walked to see them.

Read the directions to children. Guide them through the page or have them finish it independently.

Name _____

Read the words in the box. Write the word that goes with the set of pictures on each line.

cow	duck
green	red

1. _____

2. _____

3. _____

4. _____

 Read the directions to children. Guide them through the page or have them finish it independently.

Name _____

An **asking sentence** asks about something or someone. It begins with a capital letter. It ends with a question mark (?).

Write each asking sentence correctly.

1. do you see a horse

_____

- - - - - - - - - - - - - - - - - - -

_____

2. can you see a pig

_____

- - - - - - - - - - - - - - - - - - -

_____

3. will the cow play

_____

- - - - - - - - - - - - - - - - - - -

_____

4. is the cat walking

_____

- - - - - - - - - - - - - - - - - - -

_____

 Read the directions to children. Guide them through the page or have them finish it independently.

Name _____

Read the sentence and write the letter d̲, g̲, or t̲ to complete each word. Draw a line to the picture that the sentence goes with.

_ _ _ _ _ _ _

1. What is in the ba_____?

_ _ _ _
_ _ _ _

2. Is it a do_____?

_ _ _ _ _ _ _

3. Do you see the ta_____ on it?

_ _ _ _ _ _ _

4. Do you see the ha_____?

_ _ _ _
_ _ _ _

5. The hat is green and re_____.

☞ Read the directions to children. Guide them through the page or have them finish it independently.

I Went Walking

Name _____

Read each sentence and the words below it.
Write the word that best completes each sentence.

1. Do you see the _____?

   fox   pan

2. He is _____.

   hat   hot

3. He can not _____.

   nap   not

4. He got a _____.

   fan   fox

5. Fox _____ nap.

   cab   can

☞ Read the directions to children. Guide them through the page or
have them finish it independently.

   Practice Book ▪ **WHISPER A SONG**

Name _____

Look at the picture. Read each sentence and the words below it. Write the word that best completes each sentence.

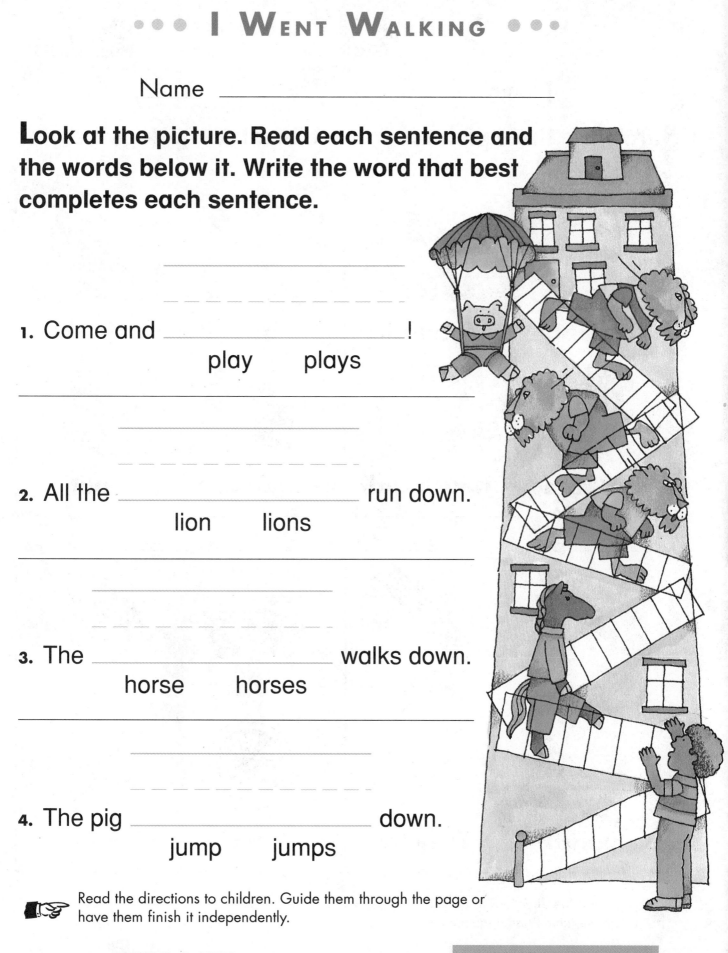

1. Come and _____!

   play   plays

2. All the _____ run down.

   lion   lions

3. The _____ walks down.

   horse   horses

4. The pig _____ down.

   jump   jumps

👉 Read the directions to children. Guide them through the page or have them finish it independently.

Name _____

Circle the three pictures in each box that go together.

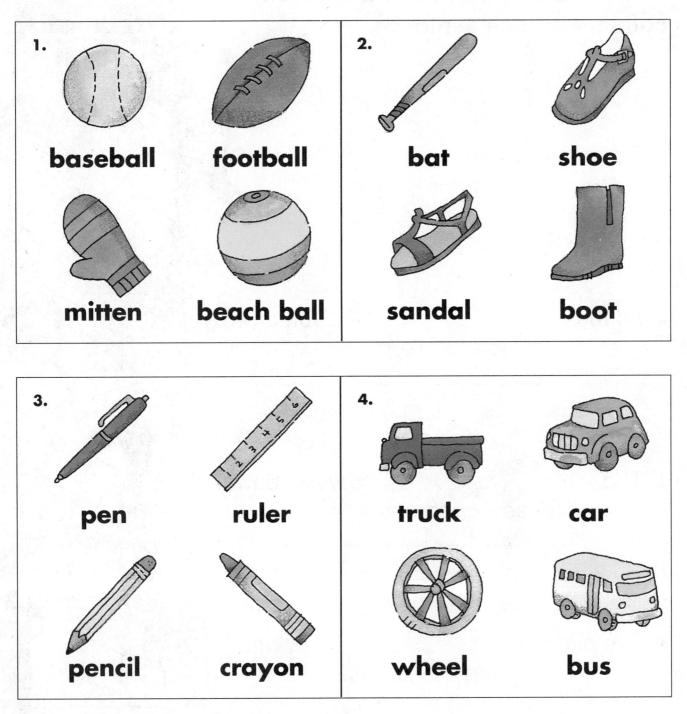

1.

baseball   football

mitten   beach ball

2.

bat   shoe

sandal   boot

3.

pen   ruler

pencil   crayon

4.

truck   car

wheel   bus

☞ Read the directions to children. Guide them through the page or have them finish it independently.

JUMP
RIGHT
IN

Name _____

**Think about the story. Read each
sentence and the words below it. Write
the word that tells about the story.**

_____

1. What can Duck and Frog _____?

   walk   play

_____

2. Duck and Frog go to see _____.

   Lion   Fox

_____

3. Duck, Frog, Fox, _____, Rabbit, and Squirrel
   go to see Owl.   Mouse   Cow

_____

4. What did _____ want to play?

   down   Owl

Read the directions to children. Guide them through the page or
have them finish it independently.

HBJ material copyrighted under notice appearing earlier in this work.

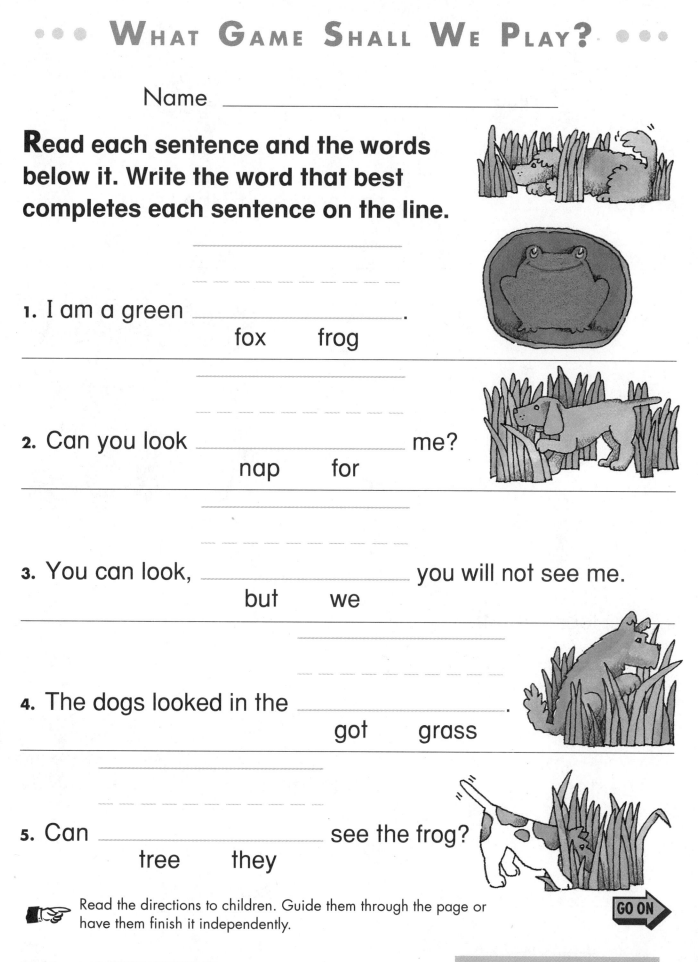

WHAT GAME SHALL WE PLAY?

Name _____

Read each sentence and the words below it. Write the word that best completes each sentence on the line.

1. I am a green _____.

   fox   frog

2. Can you look _____ me?

   nap   for

3. You can look, _____ you will not see me.

   but   we

4. The dogs looked in the _____.

   got   grass

5. Can _____ see the frog?

   tree   they

☞ Read the directions to children. Guide them through the page or have them finish it independently.

GO ON

Name _____

_____

6. "No, _____ can not see it!" they said.
          walk   we

_____

7. "I will look," _____ the cat.
          she   said

_____ "

8. "I will look up in the _____.
          tree   down

_____

9. The frog _____ in the log.
          yes   was

Name _____

Write the naming part of each sentence.

1. A frog jumped in the grass.

2. A cat saw the frog.

3. A dog saw the cat.

4. The cat jumped in the tree.

☞ Read the directions to children. Guide them through the page or have them finish it independently.

9

WHAT GAME SHALL WE PLAY?

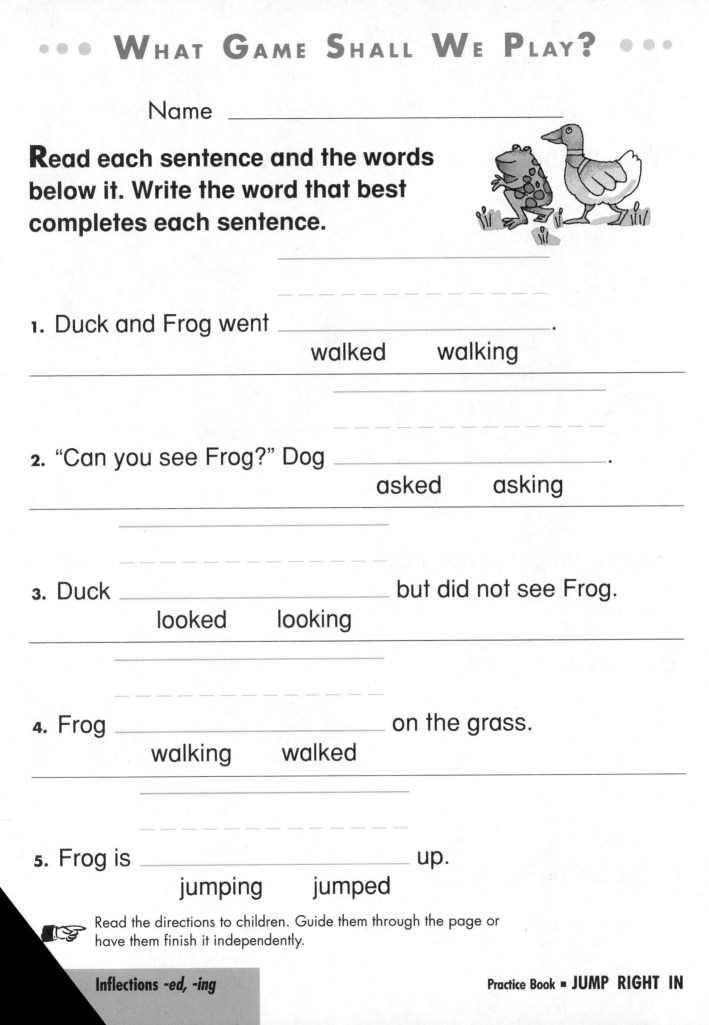

Name _____

Read each sentence and the words below it. Write the word that best completes each sentence.

1. Duck and Frog went _____ .

   walked   walking

2. "Can you see Frog?" Dog _____ .

   asked   asking

3. Duck _____ but did not see Frog.

   looked   looking

4. Frog _____ on the grass.

   walking   walked

5. Frog is _____ up.

   jumping   jumped

👉 Read the directions to children. Guide them through the page or have them finish it independently.

Inflections -ed, -ing

Name _____

Name the picture and read the sentence.
Write the letters <u>fr</u>, <u>gr</u>, or <u>tr</u> to complete
the word.

1. Can I have the _____uit?

2. Can I go up the _____ee?

3. Look at the _____een grass.

4. Look at the green _____og.

 Read the directions to children. Guide them through the page or
have them finish it independently.

Name _____

Read each sentence and the words below it. Write the word that best completes each sentence.

1. Do you see the play _____?

                men   my

2. We will play all _____.

      walking   morning

3. _____ are you?

      How   Cow

4. I _____ happy.

      from   am

☞ Read the directions to children. Guide them through the pages or have them finish independently.

GO ON ➜

Name _____

5. What will they do _____ morning?
 he   this

6. They went _____ .
 asked   away

7. _____ did they go?
 Where   Will

8. _____ they _____ !
 Here   Tree   up   are

Name _____

Write a name from the box
to complete the chart.

**Small Man
Ring Man
Pointer
Tall Man**

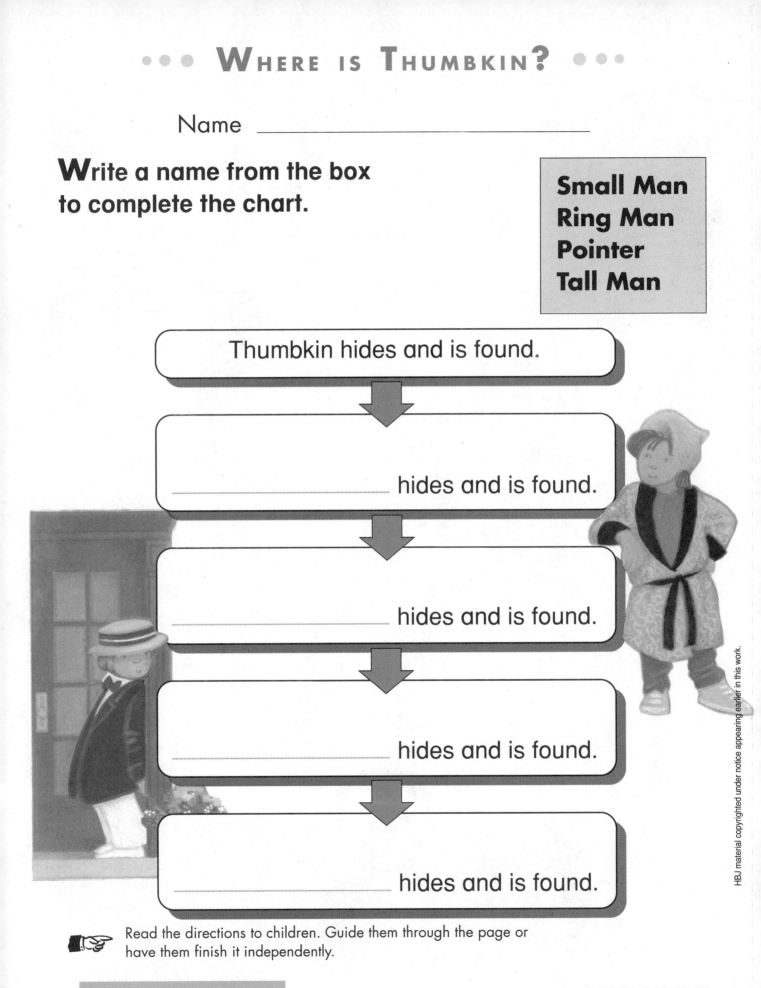

Thumbkin hides and is found.

_____ hides and is found.

_____ hides and is found.

_____ hides and is found.

_____ hides and is found.

Read the directions to children. Guide them through the page or
have them finish it independently.

••• WHERE IS THUMBKIN? •••

Name _____

Read the sentence and the words below it. Write
the word that best completes each sentence.

1. Come on, _____! Come here!

             am   men

2. Here is how we will run _____.

         away   morning

3. We will go on _____ horse.

     where   this

4. We _____ up on the horse!

   are   here

 Read the directions to children. Guide them through the page or
have them finish it independently.

Name _____

Join the naming parts of each of the two sentences. Use the word _and_. Write the new sentences.

1. A fox can run. A horse can run.

_____

_____

2. A cat can play. A dog can play.

_____

_____

3. A bird can nap. A cow can nap.

_____

_____

👉 Read the directions to children. Guide them through the page or have them finish it independently.

Name _____

Read the sentence and write the letter <u>e</u> to complete each word. Draw a line from the sentence to the picture it goes with.

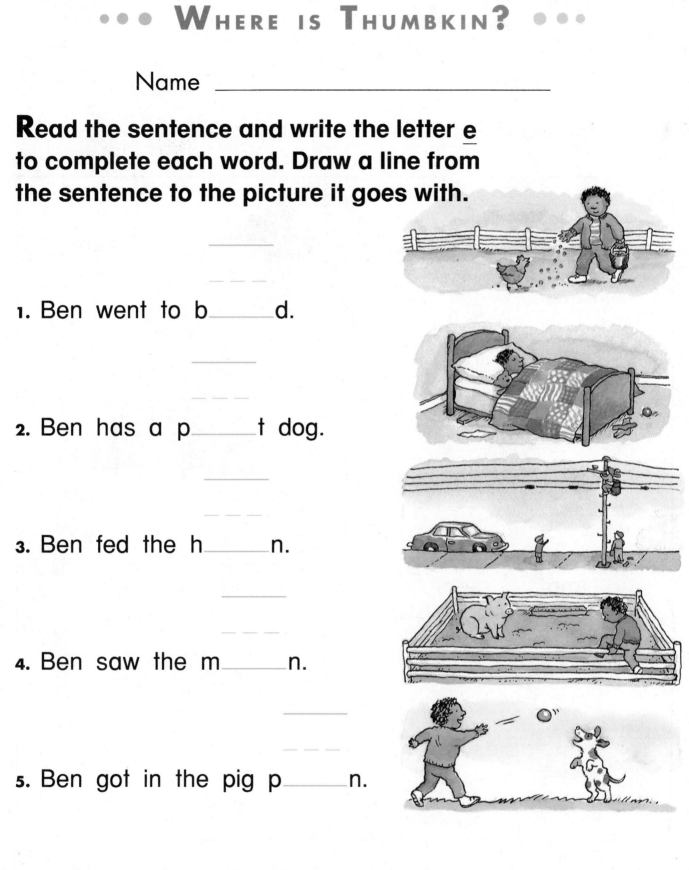

1. Ben went to b___d.

2. Ben has a p___t dog.

3. Ben fed the h___n.

4. Ben saw the m___n.

5. Ben got in the pig p___n.

👉 Read the directions to children. Guide them through the page or have them finish it independently.

Name _____

Write the word that tells about the picture.

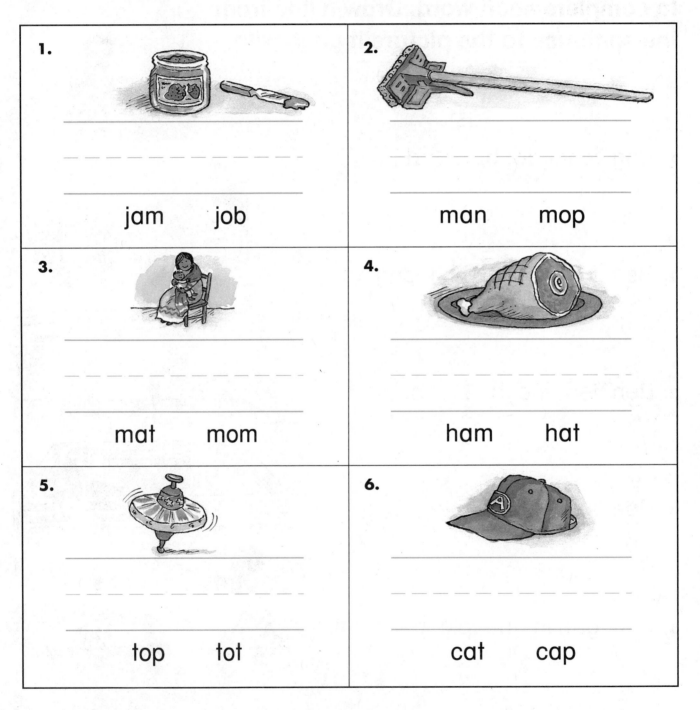

1.

jam   job

2.

man   mop

3.

mat   mom

4.

ham   hat

5.

top   tot

6.

cat   cap

👉 Read the directions to children. Guide them through the page or have them finish it independently.

Name _____

Read each sentence and the words below it. Write the word that best completes each sentence.

1. Duck _____ up to see Fox.

       walked   walking

2. "Where is Frog?" _____ Duck.

       asked   asking

3. "Did he go _____?"

       walked   walking

4. "No," Fox said. "He went _____."

       jumped   jumping

👉 Read the directions to children. Guide them through the page or have them finish it independently.

Name _____

Read each sentence and the words below it. Write the word that best completes each sentence.

_____

_ _ _ _ _ _ _ _ _ _ _ _ _ _ _ _

1. I _____ get to the tree.

      can't   are

_____

_ _ _ _ _ _ _ _ _ _ _ _ _ _ _ _

2. I _____ see how to do it.

    day   don't

_____

_ _ _ _ _ _ _ _ _ _ _ _ _ _ _ _

3. I will get _____.

      wet   went

_____

_ _ _ _ _ _ _ _ _ _ _ _ _ _ _ _

4. I can't _____ like you.

      fox   fly

_____

_ _ _ _ _ _ _ _ _ _ _ _ _ _ _ _

5. I _____ I could.

    walk   wish

☞ Read the directions to children. Guide them through the pages or have them finish independently.

GO ON

Name _____

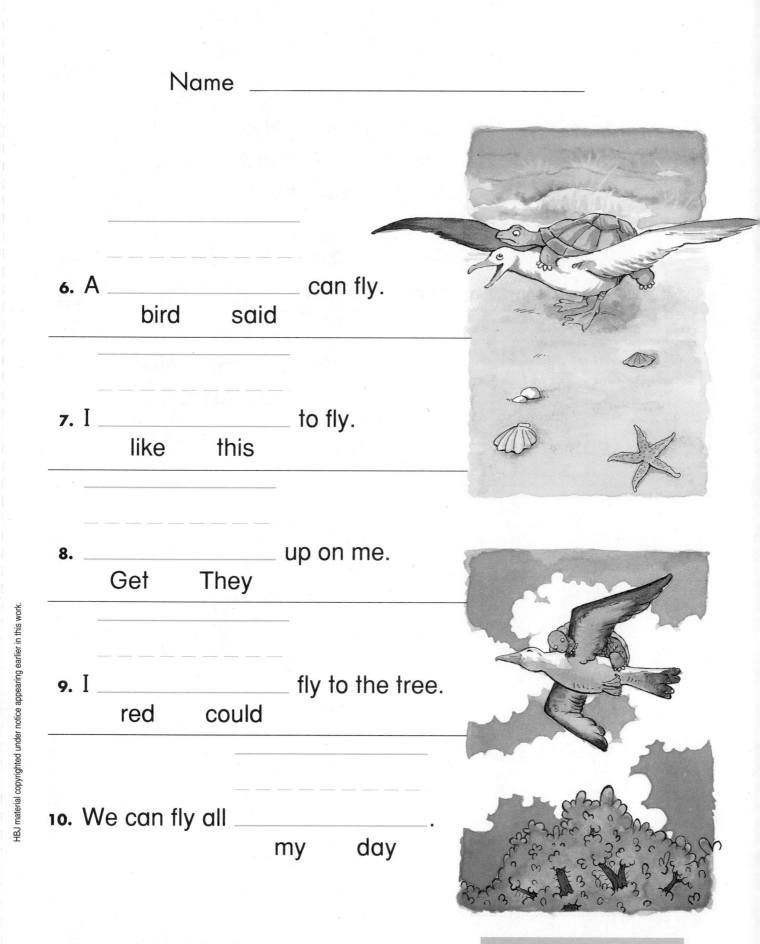

_____

6. A _____ can fly.

       bird   said

_____

7. I _____ to fly.

       like   this

_____

8. _____ up on me.

  Get   They

_____

9. I _____ fly to the tree.

    red   could

_____

10. We can fly all _____.

         my   day

Name _____

Complete the story chart by writing who Turtle saw and what he wished he could do. The words in the box will help you.

Bird	climb	Rabbit	fly
dive	Squirrel	run	Frog

Who Turtle Saw	What Turtle Wished He Could Do

☞ Read the directions to children. Guide them through the page or have them finish it independently.

Name _____

Read the words in the box. Write the word that goes with the picture.

1.

2.

sun
bird

3.

4.

like
fly

5.

6.

wet
wish

Read the directions to children. Guide them through the page or have them finish it independently.

Name _____

Write the telling part of each sentence.
Use the words in the boxes.

| is green and tall. |
| likes Pat. |
| play in the grass. |
| will play with Tom. |

_____

1. Tom _____

_____

2. Pat _____

_____

3. Pat and Tom _____

_____

4. The grass _____

👉 Read the directions to children. Guide them through the page or
have them finish it independently.

Name _____

Read each sentence and the words below it. Write the word that best completes each sentence.

1. _____ my pig?

    Bird's   Where's

2. She _____ on the grass.

    isn't   don't

3. And _____ not in here.

    she's   what's

4. She _____ go up a tree!

    couldn't   wasn't

5. _____ you see my pig?

    Don't   Isn't

👉 Read the directions to children. Guide them through the page or have them finish it independently.

Name _____

Read the sentences and the words in the boxes. Write the word that best completes each riddle.

1. You can nap on me.

_____

I am a _____.

bed	bad

2. You put a pig in me.

_____

I am a pig _____.

pin	pen

3. You can fly in me.

_____

I am a _____.

jet	jot

4. I am a dog or a cat.

_____

I could be a _____.

pet	pot

☞ Read the directions to children. Guide them through the page or have them finish it independently.

Name _____

Read each sentence and the words below it.
Write the word that best completes each sentence.

1. What is _____ ?
        grass   green

2. A _____ is green.
      frog   fog

3. A _____ is green.
      they   tree

4. The _____ is green.
     grass   pass

5. My play _____ is green, too.
       train   tan

☞ Read the directions to children. Guide them through the page or
have them finish it independently.

Name _____

Think about the story. Fill in the story map using the words in the box.

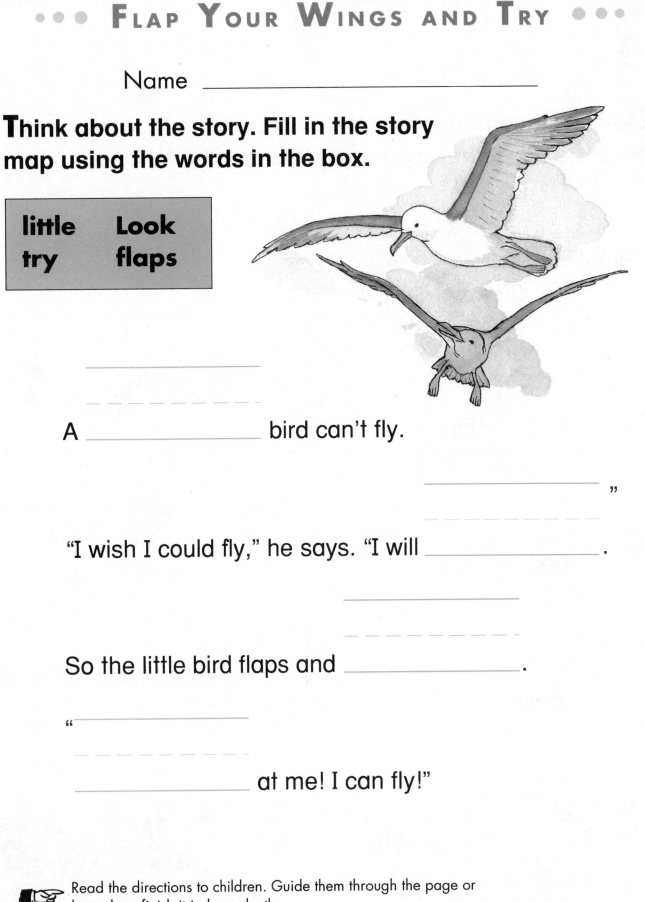

| little | Look |
| try | flaps |

_____

A _____ bird can't fly.

_____ "

_____

"I wish I could fly," he says. "I will _____.

_____

_____

So the little bird flaps and _____.

" _____

_____

_____ at me! I can fly!"

☞ Read the directions to children. Guide them through the page or have them finish it independently.

Name _____

Read each sentence and the words below it. Write the word that best completes each sentence.

1. I am a _____ bird.

   baby   jump

2. I'm _____, but I can fly.

   tree   little

3. "_____ wings let you fly," says Frog.

   Your   Tree

4. "We are not happy," the pigs _____.

   say   look

👉 Read the directions to children. Guide them through the pages or have them finish independently.

GO ON ➡

Name _____

"_____

5. _____ can't we fly?" they ask me.

   Walk   Why

_____

6. Frog and Pig say, "Let _____ see you fly."

   red   us

_____

7. I will _____ my wings and _____.

   how   flap   fly   little

_____

8. "We can't flap, _____ we can't fly."

   so   did

Name _____

Join the telling parts of each of the two sentences.
Use the word <u>and</u>. Write the new sentences.

1. Lions walk. Lions run.

_____

_ _

_____

2. Pigs play. Pigs nap.

_____

_ _

_____

3. Birds jump. Birds fly.

_____

_ _

_____

 Read the directions to children. Guide them through the page or
have them finish it independently.

Name _____

Name what Squirrel has in each box. Write the letters that are missing from the middle of the word. The letters in the box will help you.

bb	dd	ll	mm	ss	tt

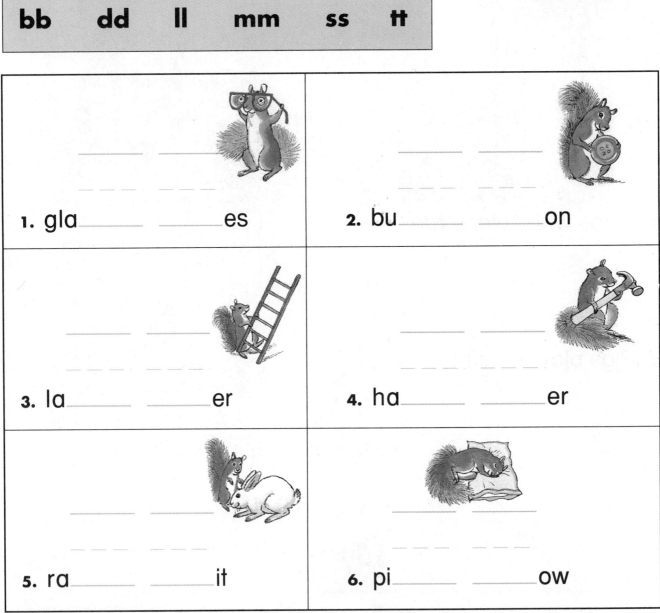

1. gla_____es

2. bu_____on

3. la_____er

4. ha_____er

5. ra_____it

6. pi_____ow

☞ Read the directions to children. Guide them through the page or have them finish it independently.

Name _____

Look at the picture and read the sentences.
Write them in order to tell the story.

My dog jumps up on me.

I say to get down.

My dog runs to me.

_____

- - - - - - - - - - - - - - - - - - - -

1. _____

_____

2. _____

- - - - - - - - - - - - - - - - - - - -

3. _____

☞ Read the directions to children. Guide them through the page or
have them finish it independently.

Name _____

Complete each sentence. Write a contraction from the box that means the same as the two words below each sentence.

He's	can't	don't	She's

1. _____ walking.
   He is

2. I _____ walk.
   can not

3. _____ flying.
   She is

4. We _____ fly.
   do not

👉 Read the directions to children. Guide them through the page or have them finish it independently.

Name _____

Read each line of the poem and the words below it. Write the word that best completes each sentence.

1. Look, _____ ! Look at what I can see!

    Mother   From

2. The _____ little ducks are up in a tree.

           six   Fox

3. _____ ducks in the tree will try, try, try.

    Not   Four

4. They will jump and flap and _____ and fly.

              quack   came

☞ Read the directions to children. Guide them through the pages or have them finish independently.

GO ON

Name _____

_____

5. _____ little duck can fly all day.

      Looked   One

_____

6. He _____ back so we could play.

    came   can

_____

7. He can fly away and come _____ .

        brown   back

_____

8. He flaps _____ me and he says "QUACK!"

    over   one

Quack!
Quack!
Quack!

Name _____

Complete the chart by writing how many ducks came back. The words and numbers in the box will help you.

0	1	2	3	4	5	6
zero	one	two	three	four	five	six

How many ducks went swimming?	How many came back?
six ducks	
five ducks	
four ducks	
three ducks	
two ducks	
one duck	

☞ Read the directions to children. Guide them through the page or have them finish it independently.

Name _____

Read the words in the box. Write a different word to complete each sentence. The picture will help you.

six	four	over	Quack	back

1. Here come _____ ducks.

2. One duck is walking _____ to me.

3. Mother Duck said, "_____"!

4. "Come _____! I see _____ cats on the grass!"

Read the directions to children. Guide them through the page or have them finish it independently.

Name _____

A sentence needs both a naming part and a telling part. Two of these groups of words are sentences. Write the two sentences.

1. The duck was swimming.

_____

- - - - - - - - - - - - - - - - - -

_____

2. The brown duck.

_____

- - - - - - - - - - - - - - - - - -

_____

3. The duck quacked.

_____

- - - - - - - - - - - - - - - - - -

_____

4. Saw the duck.

_____

- - - - - - - - - - - - - - - - - -

_____

 Read the directions to children. Guide them through the page or have them finish it independently.

Name _____

Read the words. Circle the word that names the picture. Write that word on the line.

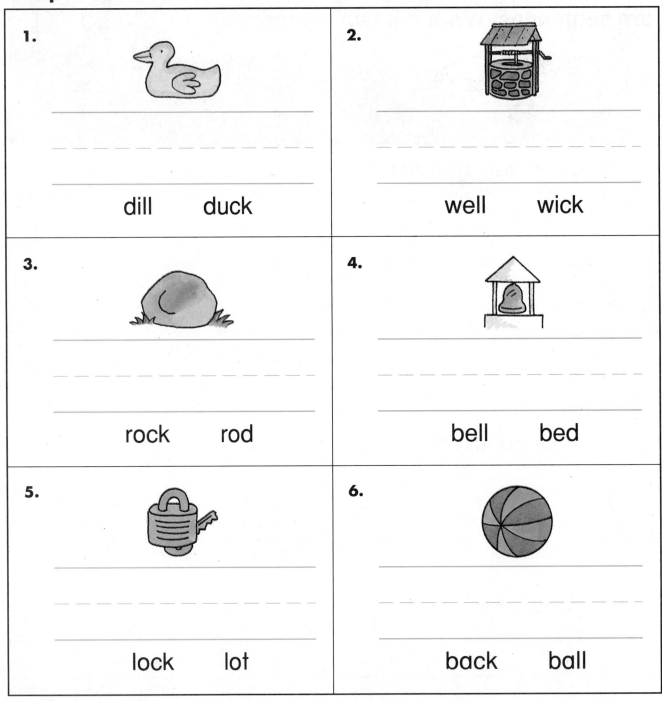

1.

_____

dill   duck

2.

_____

well   wick

3.

_____

rock   rod

4.

_____

bell   bed

5.

_____

lock   lot

6.

_____

back   ball

☞ Read the directions to children. Guide them through the page or have them finish it independently.

Name _____

Read the sentence and write the letter <u>i</u> to complete each word. Draw a line from the sentence to the picture it goes with.

1. Kit will s_____p this.

2. Kit is l_____ttle.

3. Kim sees a sh_____p.

4. Lil is s_____x.

5. Kim will put the p_____n in.

👉 Read the directions to children. Guide them through the page or have them finish it independently.

Name _____

Read the words in the box. Look at the pictures. Write the word that best completes each sentence.

quack	queen	quick	quilt

1. Jack is _____.

2. My _____ is red.

3. She is a _____.

4. A duck can _____.

👉 Read the directions to children. Guide them through the page or have them finish it independently.

Name _____

Read each sentence and the words below it. Write the word that best completes each sentence.

1. We all went _____ to play.

   don't   out

2. Pig _____ up a little grass.

   shell   pulled

3. "Can we dig a _____? asked Pig.

   hole   too

4. "It's too hot for _____," said Fox.

   how   digging

5. "Come on. We can go _____."

   six   swimming

☞ Read the directions to children. Guide them through the pages or have them finish independently.

GO ON →

Name _____

_____

6. The _____ couldn't go swimming.

    can't   chick

_____

7. She couldn't _____ at all.

    swim   away

_____

8. "Get in this _____, Chick!" said the fox.

    say   shell

9. "You will not get wet. _____"

    You can come swimming, _____.

    too   look

Name _____

Think about what happened in the story. Write a word from the box to complete the flowchart.

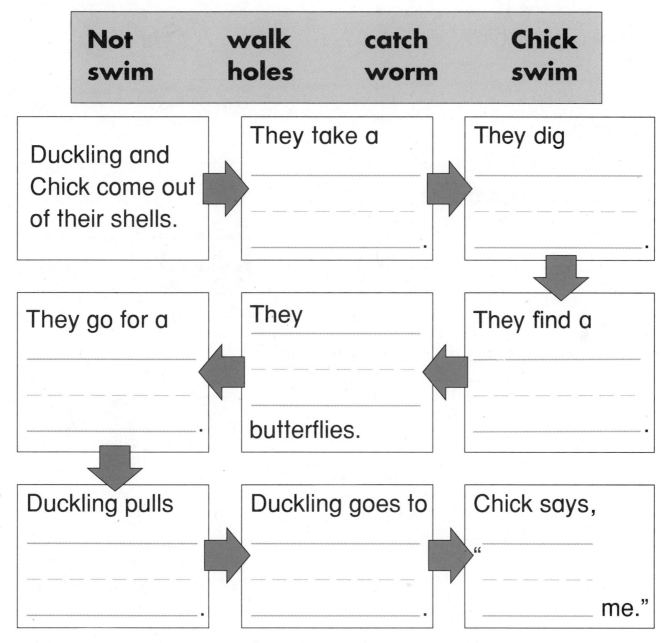

Not	walk	catch	Chick
swim	holes	worm	swim

Duckling and Chick come out of their shells.

They take a _____ .

They dig _____ .

They go for a _____ .

They _____ butterflies.

They find a _____ .

Duckling pulls _____ .

Duckling goes to _____ .

Chick says, " _____ me."

Read the directions to children. Guide them through the page or have them finish it independently.

Name _____

Read the sentences and the words in the boxes. Write the word that best completes each riddle.

1. I am a baby bird.

I am a _____ .

| chick | swim |

2. A chick comes out of me.

I am a _____ .

| pulled | shell |

3. You can see me if you are digging.

I am a _____ .

| hole | out |

4. When I do this, I get wet.

I go _____ .

| swimming | wish |

👉 Read the directions to children. Guide them through the page or have them finish it independently.

Name _____

The word **I** is always written as a capital letter. Write each sentence correctly.

1. Mother and i like to swim.

_____

_ _ _ _ _ _ _ _ _ _ _ _ _ _ _ _ _ _

_____

2. My dog and i go digging.

_____

_ _ _ _ _ _ _ _ _ _ _ _ _ _ _ _ _ _

_____

3. The shell i see is big.

_____

_ _ _ _ _ _ _ _ _ _ _ _ _ _ _ _ _ _

_____

4. Mother said i can have it.

_____

_ _ _ _ _ _ _ _ _ _ _ _ _ _ _ _ _ _

_____

 Read the directions to children. Guide them through the page or have them finish it independently.

Name _____

Read each sentence and the words below it.
Write the word that best completes each sentence.

1. What a day!

   _____

   Duck _____ so he could fly.
   flapping   flapped

2. He went _____.
   swim   swimming

3. He got hot _____ a hole.
   dig   digging

4. Duck went _____ back to the grass.
   run   running

5. Then Duck _____ a bit.
   napped   napping

👉 Read the directions to children. Guide them through the page or
have them finish it independently.

Name _____

Read the sentence and the words below
it. Write the word that best completes
each sentence.

_____

1. What is _____ ?
           wish   this

_____

2. Get _____ and see.
      will   in

_____

3. It looks like a _____ .
          pig   did

_____

4. I _____ put it on for the play.
      will   in

☛ Read the directions to children. Guide them through the page or
have them finish it independently.

Name _____

Look at the pictures and read the sentences.
Write the sentences in order to tell the story.

The chick can try to fly.

I saw an egg.

A chick came out.

I saw a hole in the shell.

1. _____

2. _____

3. _____

4. _____

 Read the directions to children. Guide them through the page or
have them finish it independently.

Name _____

Read the sentences and the words. Write
the word that best completes each sentence.

1. "I have a frog for you."

_____

- - - - - - - - - - - - - -

"I _____ you can't see it."

      bet   but

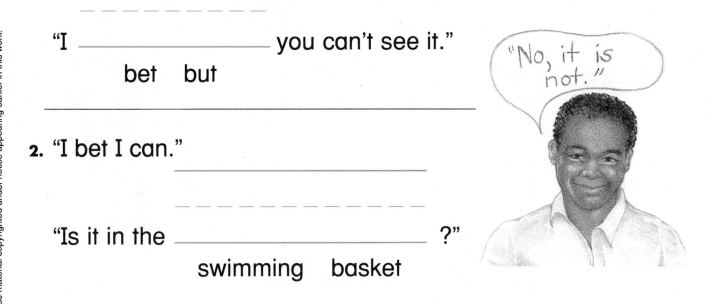

"No, it is not."

2. "I bet I can."

_____

- - - - - - - - - - - - - -

"Is it in the _____ ?"

     swimming   basket

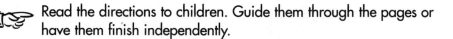

Read the directions to children. Guide them through the pages or
have them finish independently.

Name _____

_____
- - - - - - - - -

3. "I will _____ up."
       could   clean

_____

"_____
- - - - - - -

4. _____ I will see it."
   Then   He

_____

"_____
- - - - - - -

5. _____ this."
   Lion   Lift

_____

"_____
- - - - - - -

6. _____, do you like the frog?"
   Was   Well

"Yes, I like it."

Name _____

Write a word group from the box to complete the sentences about the story.

can't lift	clean up
get into	the basket

_____

_____

She lifts _____.

_____

_____

He _____ the basket.

_____

_____

They _____ the basket.

_____

_____

They _____.

Read the directions to children. Guide them through the page or have them finish it independently.

Name _____

Read each sentence and the words in the box. Write the word that best completes the sentence.

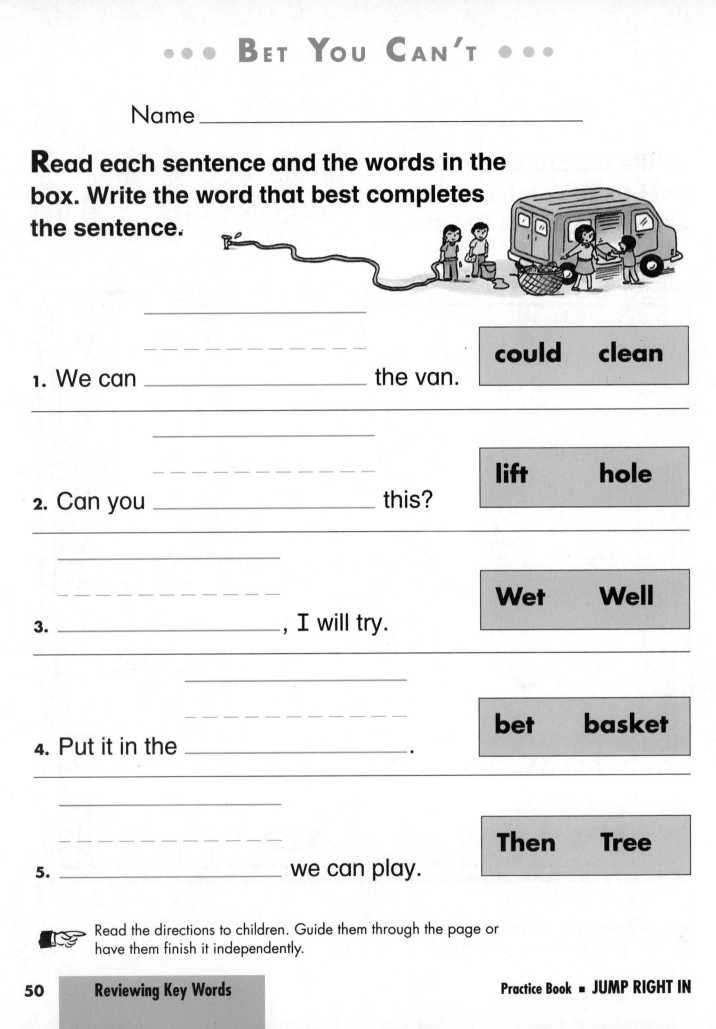

1. We can _____ the van.

could	clean

2. Can you _____ this?

lift	hole

3. _____, I will try.

Wet	Well

4. Put it in the _____.

bet	basket

5. _____ we can play.

Then	Tree

☞ Read the directions to children. Guide them through the page or have them finish it independently.

Name _____

A telling sentence ends with a period (.).

An asking sentence ends with a question mark (?).

A sentence that shows strong feeling ends with an exclamation point (!).

Write each sentence. Use the correct end mark.

1. What can I do

_____

- -

_____

2. You can get the basket

_____

- -

_____

3. Look out for the basket

_____

- -

_____

☞ Read the directions to children. Guide them through the page or have them finish it independently.

Name _____

Read the words. Circle the word that names
the picture. Write that word on the line.

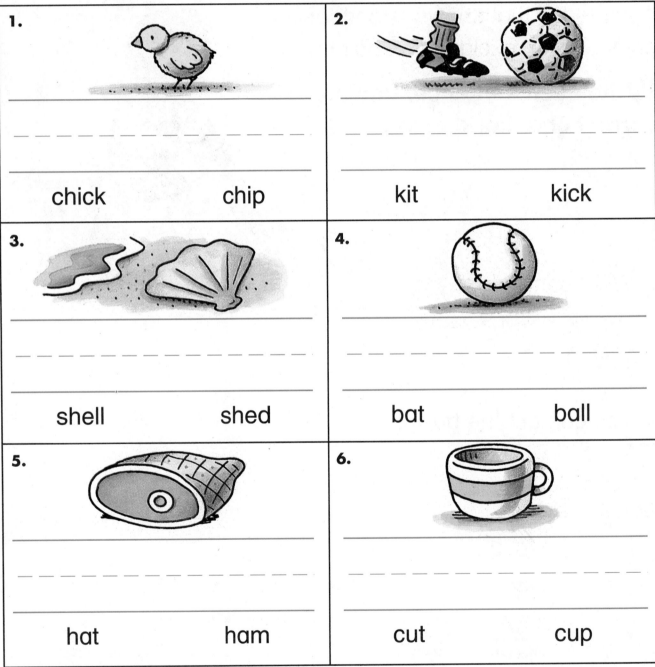

1.

_____

chick   chip

2.

_____

kit   kick

3.

_____

shell   shed

4.

_____

bat   ball

5.

_____

hat   ham

6.

_____

cut   cup

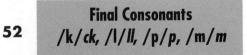

Read the directions to children. Guide them through the page or
have them finish it independently.

Name _____

Read each sentence and the words below it.
Write the word that best completes each sentence.

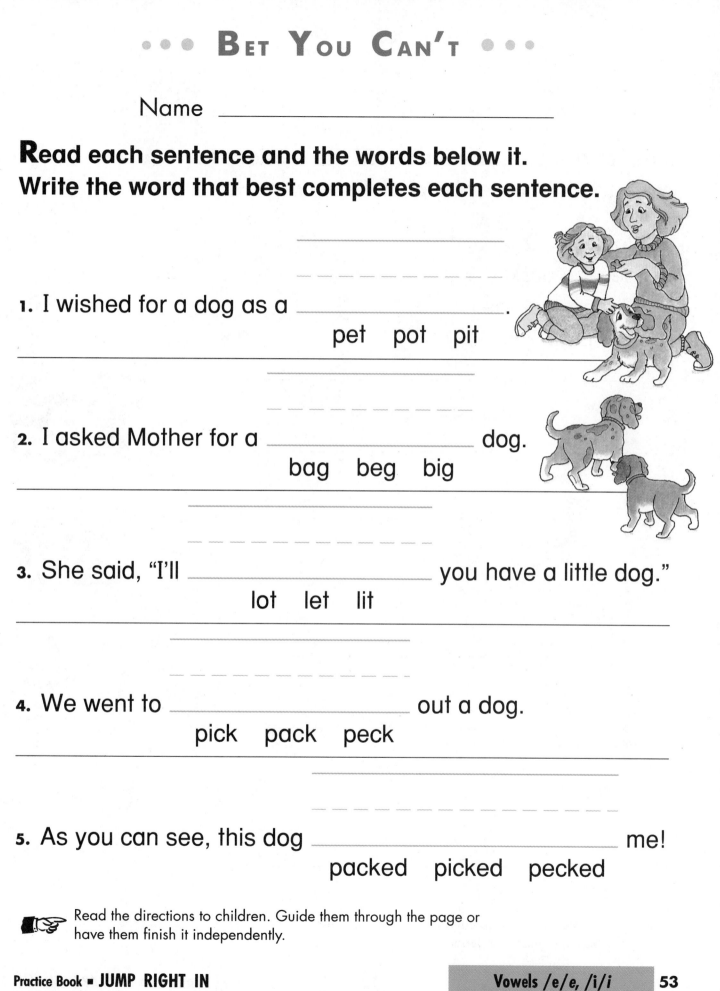

1. I wished for a dog as a _____.

   pet   pot   pit

2. I asked Mother for a _____ dog.

   bag   beg   big

3. She said, "I'll _____ you have a little dog."

   lot   let   lit

4. We went to _____ out a dog.

   pick   pack   peck

5. As you can see, this dog _____ me!

   packed   picked   pecked

☞ Read the directions to children. Guide them through the page or
have them finish it independently.

Name _____

Look at the pictures and read the sentences.
Write them in order to tell the story.

I look in.
I see the basket.
No one sees me.
I jump in.

☞ Read the directions to children. Guide them through the page or
have them finish it independently.

COLOR
THE
SKY

Name _____

In "Together," what things did the girls do?
List those things on the chart. Use the
pictures to help.

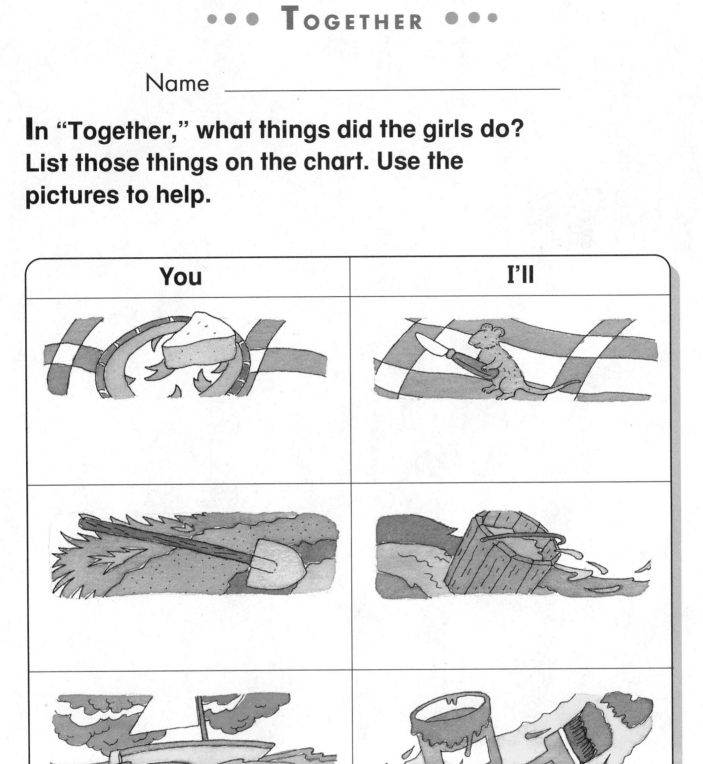

You	I'll

Read the directions to children. Guide them through the page or
have them finish it independently.

Name _____

Read each sentence and the words below it. Write the word that best completes each sentence.

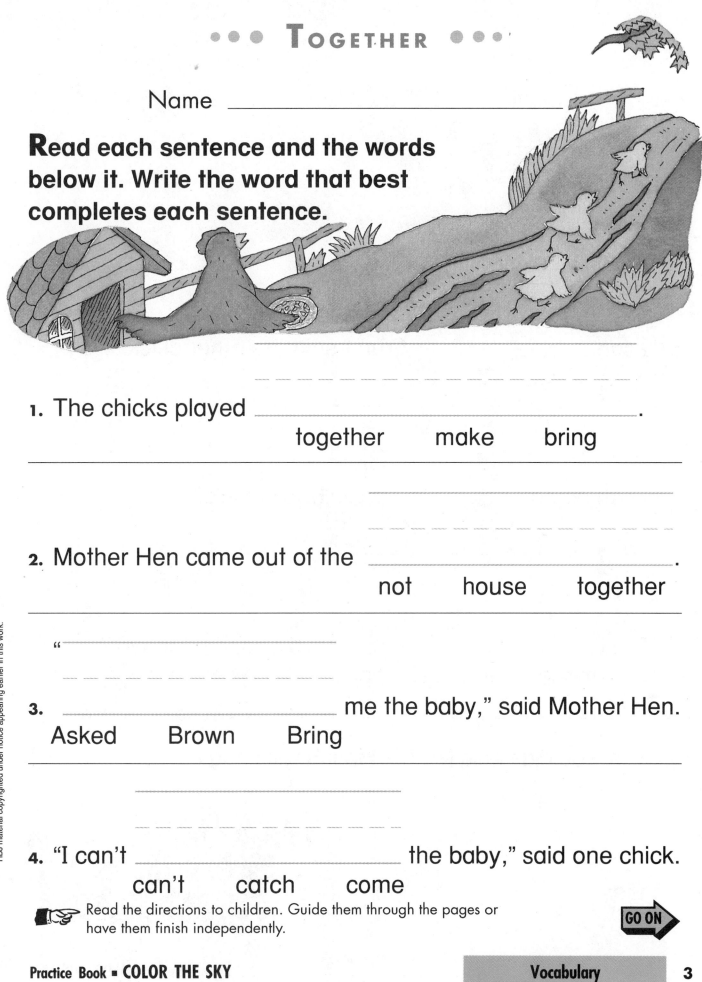

1. The chicks played _____.

       together   make   bring

2. Mother Hen came out of the _____.

       not   house   together

3. "_____ me the baby," said Mother Hen.

  Asked   Brown   Bring

4. "I can't _____ the baby," said one chick.

    can't   catch   come

☞ Read the directions to children. Guide them through the pages or have them finish independently.

GO ON ➡

Name _____

_____

5. "I can _____ I run," said the other chick.

       house   if   I'll

_____

6. "I can catch _____ baby chick."

       try   our   if

_____

7. "Did I _____ you happy, Mother?"

      make   happy   back

8. "Yes, you did," said Mother Hen. "I will bring us

_____"

_____.

cheese   make   quack

Name _____

Write the word in each sentence that is a naming word.

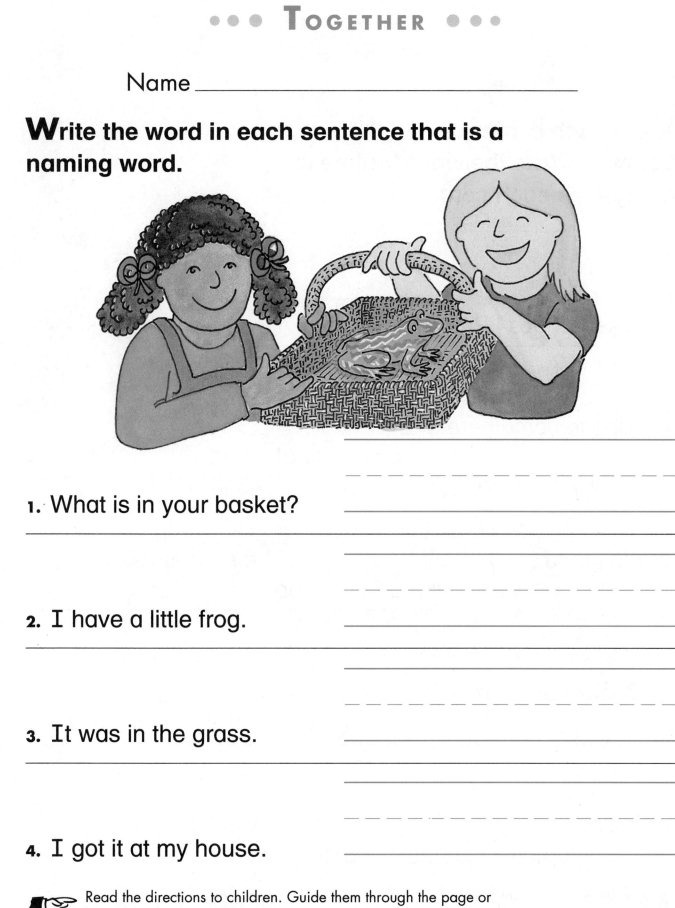

_____

- - - - - - - - - - - - - - -

1. What is in your basket?   _____

_____

- - - - - - - - - - - - - - -

2. I have a little frog.   _____

_____

- - - - - - - - - - - - - - -

3. It was in the grass.   _____

_____

- - - - - - - - - - - - - - -

4. I got it at my house.   _____

☞ Read the directions to children. Guide them through the page or have them finish it independently.

Name _____

Read each sentence and the words below it. Write the word that best completes each sentence.

" _____
_____

1. _____ can't swim," said Chick.
Chicks   Chops   Patch

_____ "

2. "I like to come here and _____ .
chip   chat   chin

_____

3. "It's fun to _____ the others swim."
rich   watch   chop

_____ "

4. "Ducks can swim when they _____ .
hatch   much   cheese

_____

5. "I can't _____ up with Duck."
patch   chap   catch

☞ Read the directions to children. Guide them through the page or have them finish it independently.

Name _____

Read each sentence and the two words below it. Write a word from the box that stands for the two words.

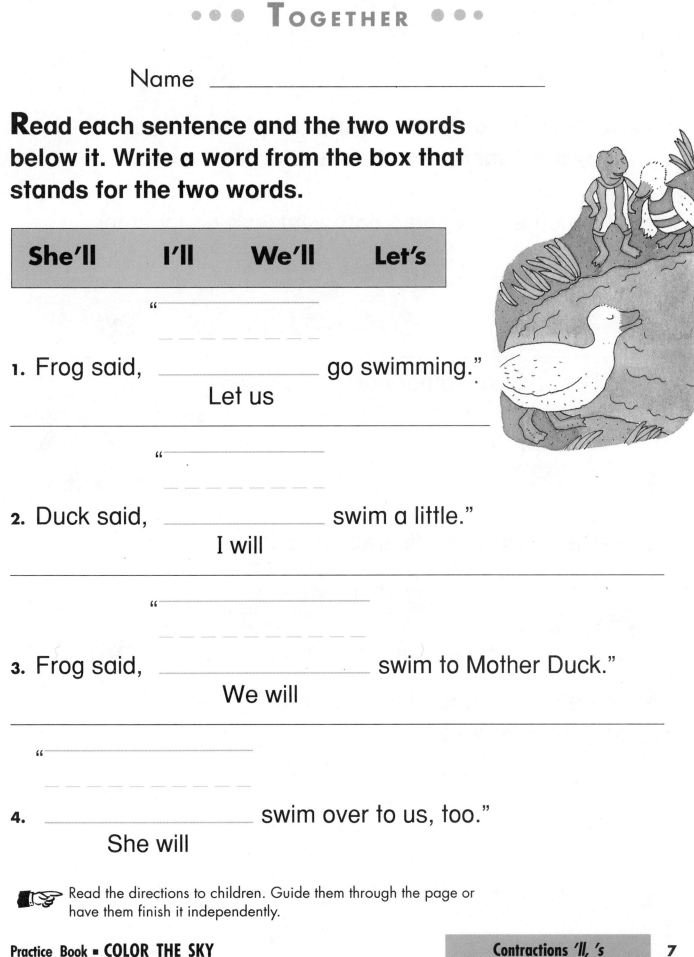

She'll	I'll	We'll	Let's

1. Frog said, " _____ go swimming."
   Let us

2. Duck said, " _____ swim a little."
   I will

3. Frog said, " _____ swim to Mother Duck."
   We will

4. " _____ swim over to us, too."
   She will

☞ Read the directions to children. Guide them through the page or have them finish it independently.

Name _____

A. Read each sentence. Circle the picture that shows the meaning of the underlined word.

1. A mother cow and a <u>calf</u> went walking together.

2. They saw a mother horse and a <u>foal</u>.

3. They saw six ducks swimming in the <u>lake</u>.

B. Write a sentence of your own using one of the underlined words.

_____

_____

_____

👉 Read the directions to children. Guide them through the page or have them finish it independently.

Name _____

Read each sentence and the words below it. Write the word that best completes each sentence.

1. Ted _____ a little nap and had a dream.
   asked   took   looked

2. "What a _____ dream!" he said as he got up.
   good   fly   shell

3. "I was swimming with _____ frogs and a dog."
   horse   quack   five

4. "One _____ frog came to swim."
   this   jump   more

👉 Read the directions to children. Guide them through the pages or have them finish independently.

GO ON ➡

Name _____

_____

5. "A mother hen took out _____ cheese."

        looked   horse   her

_____ "

_____

6. "She said we could have it _____ .

        grass   hen   now

_____ "

_____

7. "A fox took the cheese in his _____ .

        me   us   teeth

_____

8. "He ran _____ with it."

     thank   play   off

_____

9. "The fox didn't say _____ you!"

     thank   not   put

Name _____

Fill in the chart for "Five Little Monkeys" by drawing the monkeys and writing the number that tells how many.

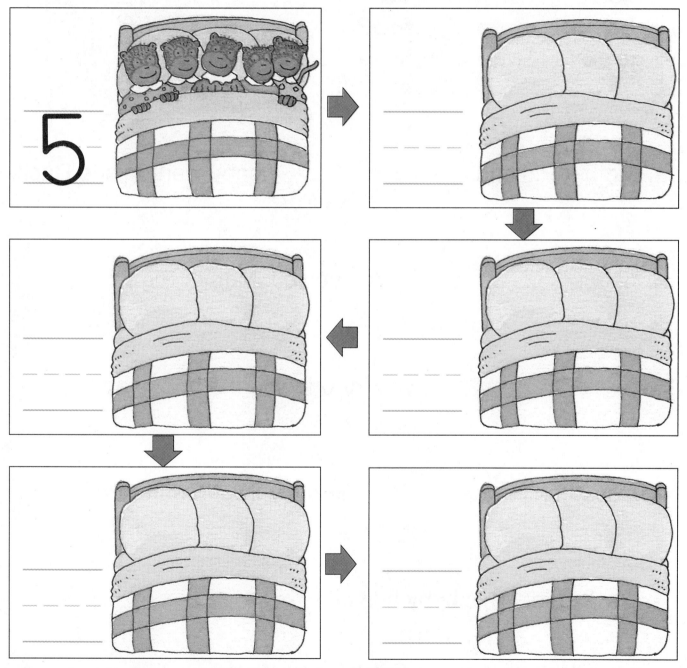

Read the directions to children. Guide them through the page or have them finish it independently.

Name _____

Read each sentence. Write a word from the box to complete each one.

teeth	her	off
five	more	took
good	Thank	now

1. Mother Pig and _____ baby went to see Duck.

2. "It is _____ to see you, Mother Pig," said Duck.

3. _____ you for bringing the baby, too."

4. Duck _____ the baby from Mother Pig.

5. Duck said, "This baby has five _____ !

👉 Read the directions to children. Guide them through the page or have them finish it independently.

Name _____

A. Read each sentence. Write the word in each sentence that names people.

1. Five men are digging. _____

2. My mother is in the house. _____

3. The baby is happy. _____

4. Four friends are jumping. _____

☞ Read the directions to children. Guide them through the page or have them finish it independently.

GO ON ➡

Name _____

B. Imagine that you see four people while
on a walk. Complete each line with
a naming word that names people.

As I went walking out one day,
I saw four people on my way:

_____

a _____,

_____

a _____,

_____

a _____,

_____

and a _____.

Name _____

Read each sentence and the words below it. Write the word that best completes the sentence and goes with the picture.

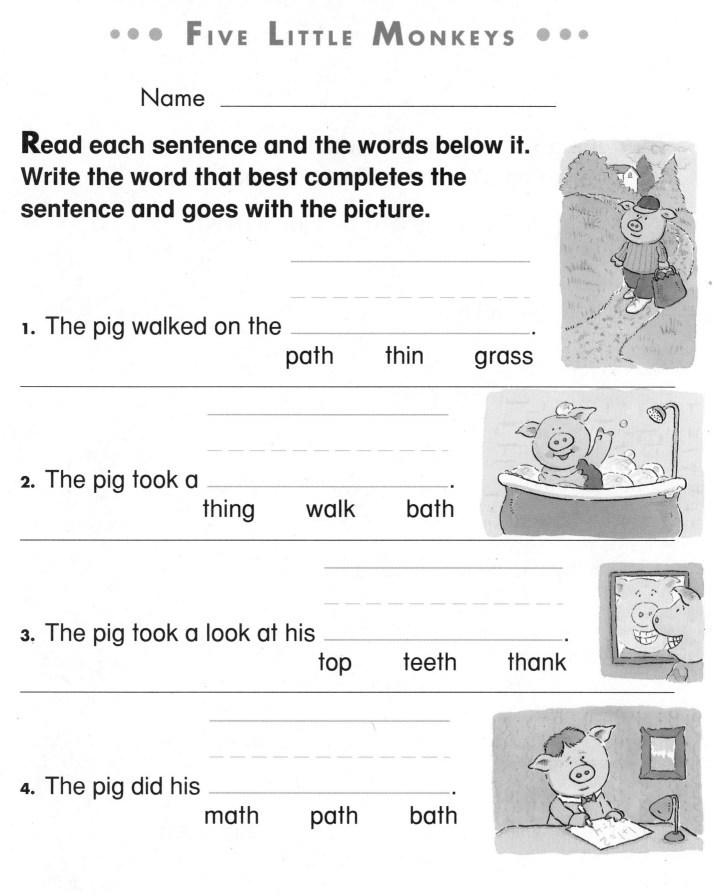

1. The pig walked on the _____.

         path   thin   grass

2. The pig took a _____.

    thing   walk   bath

3. The pig took a look at his _____.

     top   teeth   thank

4. The pig did his _____.

    math   path   bath

👉 Read the directions to children. Guide them through the page or have them finish it independently.

Name _____

Read the groups of sentences. Write the word
that best completes the last sentence.

1. The dog is happy. The dog is digging deep.

_____

The dog will make a _____.

                       frog   hole

2. Bob was dreaming. Now it is morning.

"_____

Mother said, _____, Bob."

            Get up   Good luck

3. The baby bird wants to get out of the

_____

tree. She wants to _____.

            swim   fly

4. Nan asked Maria to come over. Maria said yes.

_____

Now they will _____ together.

           play   quack

☞ Read the directions to children. Guide them through the page or
have them finish it independently.

Name _____

Read the sentences in each box. Follow the directions using crayons or colored markers.

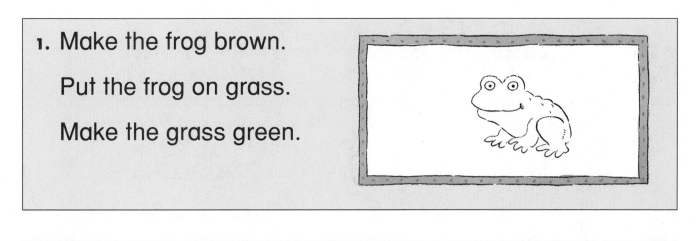

1. Make the frog brown.

   Put the frog on grass.

   Make the grass green.

2. Make Jim look happy.

   Put a tree where you like.

3. What makes you happy?

   Put it here.

Read the directions to children. Guide them through the page or have them finish it independently.

Name _____

Read the words in the box and look at each picture. Write the word that names the baby animal.

calf	chick	cub	pup	fawn

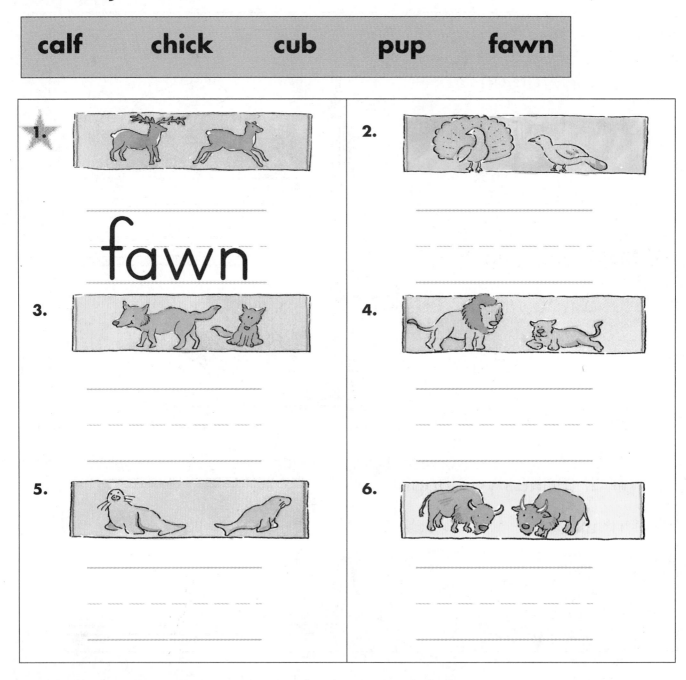

1. ⭐

fawn

2.

3.

4.

5.

6.

👉 Read the directions to children. Guide them through the page or have them finish it independently.

••• WHOSE BABY? •••

Name _____

Read each sentence and the words below it. Write the word that best completes each sentence.

_____

1. Cow and her baby _____ came to see Fox.

   frog   calf   tree

_____

_____ "

2. "Where is your baby _____? asked Cow.

   duck   shell   cub

_____

_____ "

3. "My baby is _____, said Fox.

   morning   asleep   mother

_____

_____ "

4. "When will she be _____? asked Cow.

   awake   other   four

☞ Read the directions to children. Guide them through the pages or have them finish independently.

GO ON ➡

Name _____

5. Now the baby fox was _____ awake.

wide   why   whose

6. They all went to see Dog and his _____.

nap   pup   quack

7. They went running _____ together.

fast   digging   cheese

8. "I'm so happy to be a _____," said Dog.

now   father   horse

9. "My baby _____ to me!"

belongs   now   you

Name _____

A. Look at each picture. Write the word
that names a place.

1. farm   horse

_____

- - - - - - - - - - - - - -

_____

2. flag   school

_____

- - - - - - - - - - - - - -

_____

3. green   house

_____

- - - - - - - - - - - - - -

_____

4. pond   duck

_____

- - - - - - - - - - - - - -

_____

 Read the directions to children. Guide them through the page or
have them finish it independently.

 GO ON

Name _____

B. Read the sentences in the story. Complete each sentence with the correct naming word from the box.

| fox | teeth | tree | cub |

_____

- - - - - - - - - - - - - - - - -

1. We saw a lion and its _____ .

_____

- - - - - - - - - - - - - - - - -

2. The cub was by a _____ .

_____

- - - - - - - - - - - - - - - - -

3. Then we saw a _____ .

_____

- - - - - - - - - - - - - - - - -

4. The fox had lots of _____ .

☞ Read the directions to children. Guide them through the page or have them finish it independently.

Naming Words for Places, Animals, and Things

Name _____

Read each sentence and the words below it. Write the word that best completes each sentence.

_____

1. Jeff got _____ the bus.

    off   miss

_____

2. On a tree, he saw a red _____.

    calf   leaf

_____

3. Then he saw a _____, too.

    web   cab

_____

4. He looked down at the _____.

    dress   grass

_____ "

5. "I have fun when I get off the _____.

    bus   less

☞ Read the directions to children. Guide them through the page or have them finish it independently.

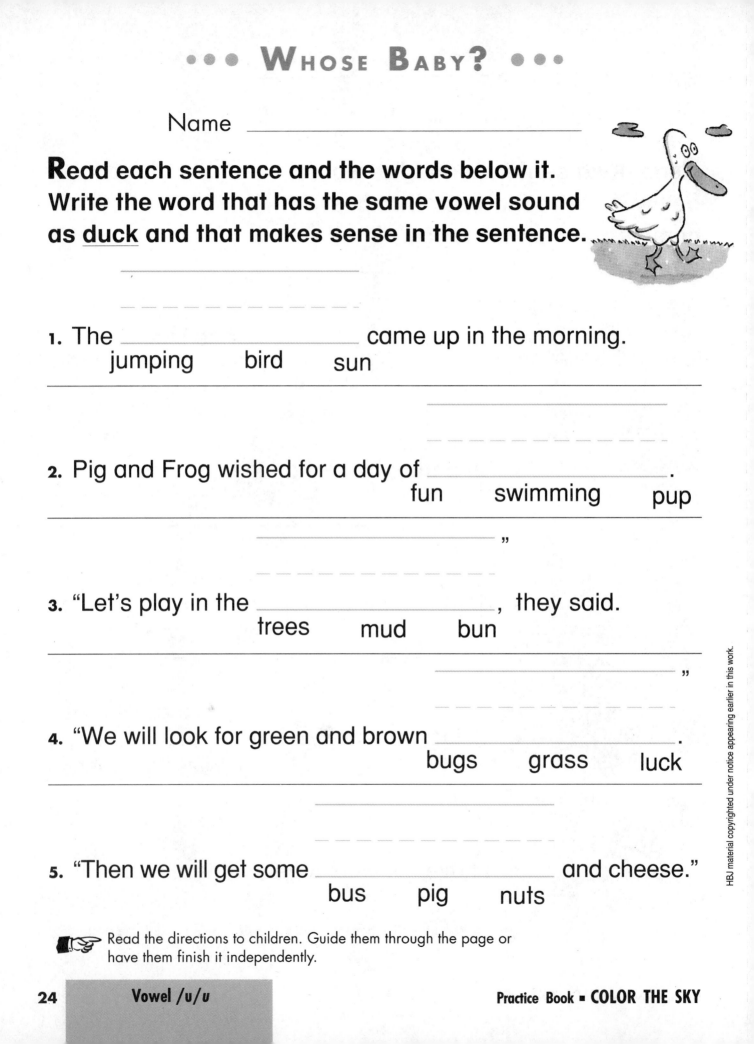

••• **WHOSE BABY?** •••

Name _____

Read each sentence and the words below it.
Write the word that has the same vowel sound
as <u>duck</u> and that makes sense in the sentence.

_____

1. The _____ came up in the morning.
   jumping   bird   sun

_____

2. Pig and Frog wished for a day of _____.
   fun   swimming   pup

_____ "

3. "Let's play in the _____, they said.
   trees   mud   bun

_____ "

4. "We will look for green and brown _____.
   bugs   grass   luck

_____

5. "Then we will get some _____ and cheese."
   bus   pig   nuts

☞ Read the directions to children. Guide them through the page or
have them finish it independently.

HBJ material copyrighted under notice appearing earlier in this work.

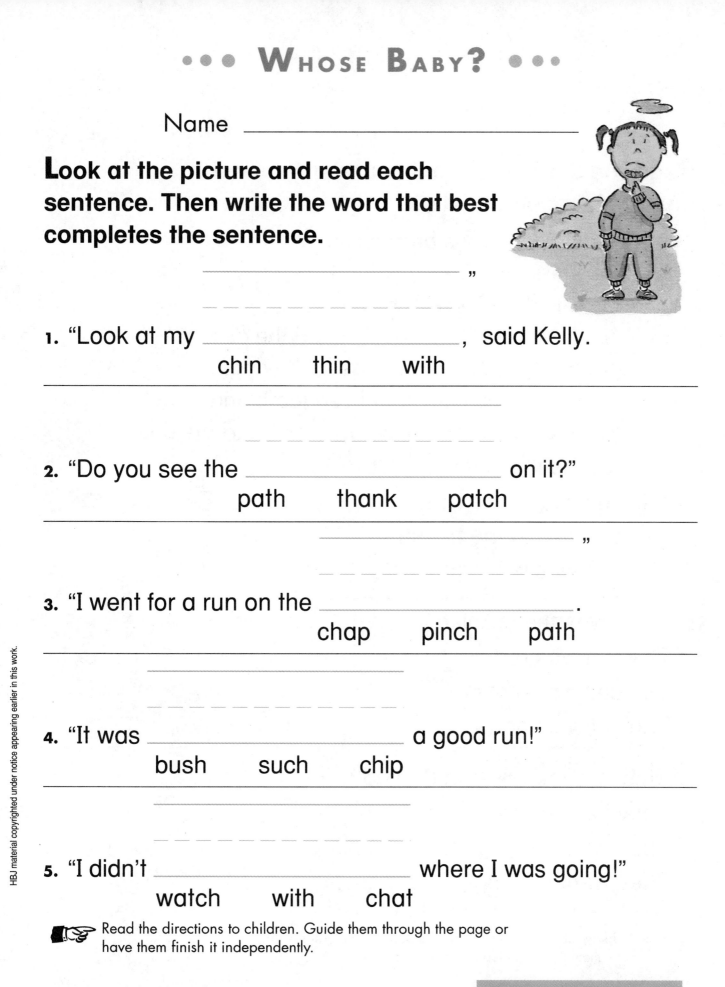

Name _____

Look at the picture and read each sentence. Then write the word that best completes the sentence.

_____ "
_ _ _ _ _ _ _ _ _ _ _ _ _ _ _ _ _

1. "Look at my _____, said Kelly.

     chin   thin   with

_ _ _ _ _ _ _ _ _ _ _ _ _ _ _ _ _

2. "Do you see the _____ on it?"

     path   thank   patch

_____ "
_ _ _ _ _ _ _ _ _ _ _ _ _ _ _ _ _

3. "I went for a run on the _____.

     chap   pinch   path

_ _ _ _ _ _ _ _ _ _ _ _ _ _ _ _ _

4. "It was _____ a good run!"

     bush   such   chip

_ _ _ _ _ _ _ _ _ _ _ _ _ _ _ _ _

5. "I didn't _____ where I was going!"

     watch   with   chat

☞ Read the directions to children. Guide them through the page or have them finish it independently.

Name _____

Read the story. Draw a line under the best answer for each question.

A little dog saw a brown calf in the grass.

He asked, "Whose baby are you?"

"I am Mother Cow's baby," said the calf.

"Can you run and dig?" asked the dog.

"No," said the calf. "But I can jump and play."

"We can jump and play together," said the dog.

1. Where was the calf?

   The calf was in the tree.

   The calf was in the house.

   The calf was in the grass.

2. What was the calf like?

   The calf was red.

   The calf was brown.

   The calf was hot.

3. What did the calf and dog do?

   They jumped and played.

   They went digging and swimming.

   They went running in the grass.

☞ Read the directions to children. Guide them through the page or have them finish it independently.

Name _____

Read each sentence and the words
below it. Write the word that
best completes each sentence.

1. "I am _____ you are here."

   get   glad

2. "Will you _____ this to me?"

   red   read

                                                    "

3. "No, I am going to set the _____ .

   then   table

4. "You can set it _____ me."

   with   wish

☞ Read the directions to children. Guide them through the pages or
   have them finish independently.

Name _____

5. "Can you do this faster _____ me?"

the   than

"

6. "No, I have to get one more _____ .

fun   fork

7. "I'm happy you did not _____ it."

drop   dog

8. "I'm happy we are _____ friends."

baby   best

Name _____

Look at each picture. Write the word from the box that tells what the best friends in the story did.

| eat | paint | read | run | climb | jump |

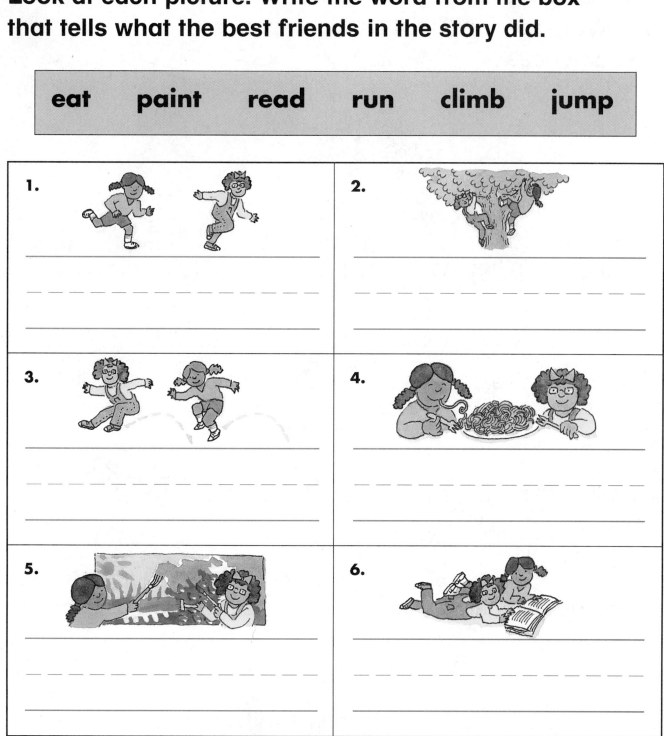

1.

2.

3.

4.

5.

6.

☞ Read the directions to children. Guide them through the page or have them finish it independently.

Name _____

Read each sentence and the words in the box. Write the word that best completes the sentence.

LIBRARY

1. I'm going in here to _____ .

read	tree

2. Will you come _____ me?

well	with

3. I will read my _____ for you.

back	best

4. We can sit at this _____ .

table	swim

5. I am _____ you came with me.

get	glad

☞ Read the directions to children. Guide them through the page or have them finish it independently.

Name _____

A. **C**omplete each sentence with the name
of a special person you know. Begin each
special name with a capital letter.

_____

- -

1. My best friend is _____.

_____

- - - - - - - - - - - - - - - - - -

2. _____ and I like to play.

_____

- -

3. I will walk with _____.

_____

- - - - - - - - - - - - - - - - - -

4. We will ask _____ to play, too.

Read the directions to children. Guide them through the page or
have them finish it independently.

GO ON

**Special Names and Titles
of People**

Name _____

B. Write the special title and name of each person correctly.

1. Our friend mrs. brown lost her bird.

_____

- - - - - - - - - - - - - - - - - - -

_____

2. She saw dr. fox at the park.

_____

- - - - - - - - - - - - - - - - - - -

_____

3. miss perez saw the bird.

_____

- - - - - - - - - - - - - - - - - - -

_____

4. She said mr. green could catch the bird.

_____

- - - - - - - - - - - - - - - - - - -

_____

Read the directions to children. Guide them through the page or have them finish it independently.

Name _____

Look at each picture and read the sentence.
If it could really happen, write <u>yes</u>.
If it could not really happen, write <u>no</u>.

1.

My friend comes to my

house. _____

2.

My house and I go to see

my friend. _____

3.

My friend and I fly over

a tree. _____

4.

My friend and I walk away

from a tree. _____

5.

Our dogs like

cheese. _____

6.

My friend and I play with

our dogs. _____

☞ Read the directions to children. Guide them through the page or
have them finish it independently.

Name _____

Read each sentence and the words below it. Write the word that best completes each sentence.

_____

1. I am playing in the _____.
   grass   good

2. We have to get on the _____.
   bet   bus

3. I will call you _____ I see it.
   at   if

4. The bus will drop us _____.
   off   up

5. Then we will walk to my _____.
   jump   job

Read the directions to children. Guide them through the page or have them finish it independently.

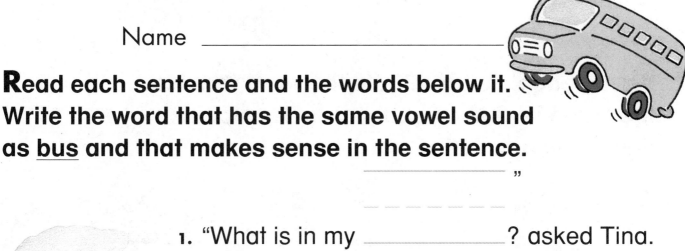

Name _____

Read each sentence and the words below it.
Write the word that has the same vowel sound
as <u>bus</u> and that makes sense in the sentence.

_____ ”

_ _ _ _ _ _ _ _ _ _ _ _ _ _

1. "What is in my _____? asked Tina.

        cup   dish   hug

_____ ”

_ _ _ _ _ _ _ _ _ _ _ _ _ _

2. "It looks like a red _____.

        fly   up   bug

_ _ _ _ _ _ _ _ _ _ _ _ _ _

3. "Are you having _____, Red Bug?"

        fun   cut   dog

_____ ”

_ _ _ _ _ _ _ _ _ _ _ _ _ _

4. "I'll put it on the _____.

        cut   rug   grass

_ _ _ _ _ _ _ _ _ _ _ _ _ _

5. "Red Bug, _____ to your house!"

        run   go   tub

Read the directions to children. Guide them through the page or
have them finish it independently.

Name _____

Name each picture. Circle the word that has the same beginning sounds as the picture name. Then write the word on the line.

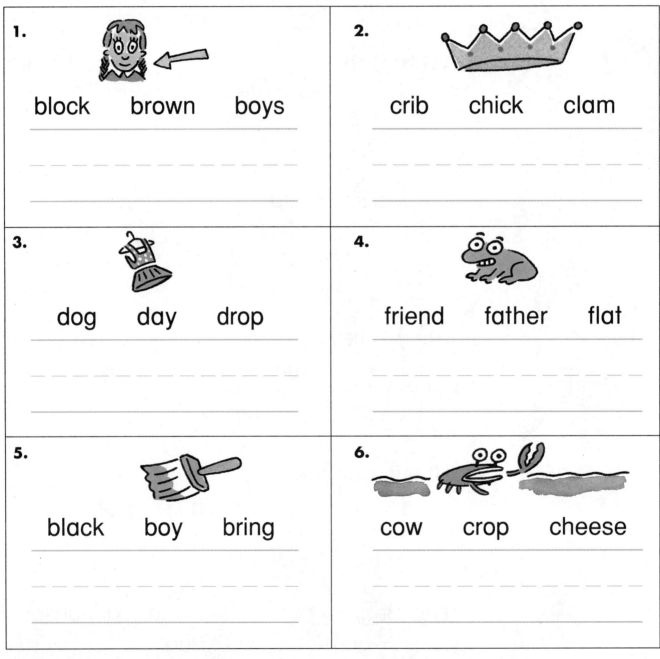

1.

block   brown   boys

_____

_____

2.

crib   chick   clam

_____

_____

3.

dog   day   drop

_____

_____

4.

friend   father   flat

_____

_____

5.

black   boy   bring

_____

_____

6.

cow   crop   cheese

_____

_____

Read the directions to children. Guide them through the page or have them finish it independently.

Name _____

Read each sentence and the words below it. Write the word that best completes each sentence.

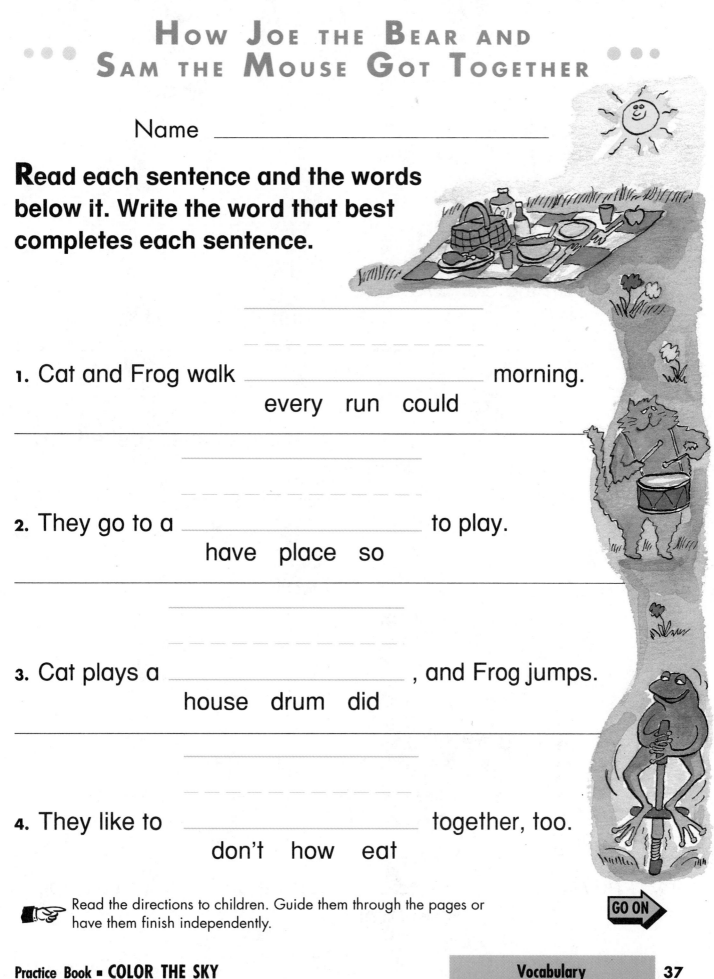

1. Cat and Frog walk _____ morning.

    every   run   could

2. They go to a _____ to play.

    have   place   so

3. Cat plays a _____ , and Frog jumps.

    house   drum   did

4. They like to _____ together, too.

    don't   how   eat

Read the directions to children. Guide them through the pages or have them finish independently.

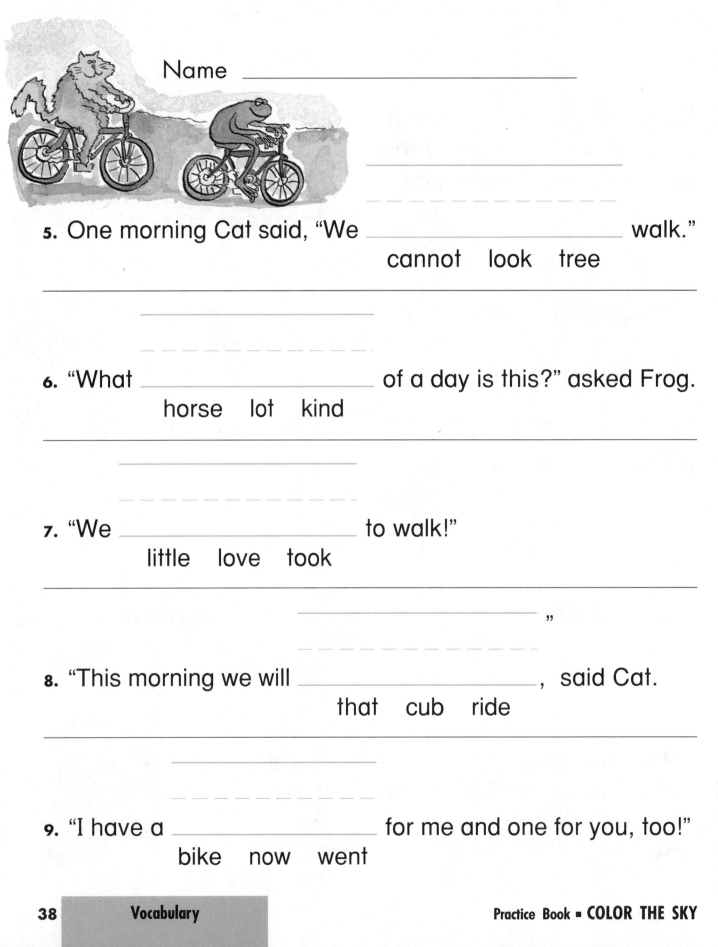

Name _____

5. One morning Cat said, "We _____ walk."

                         cannot   look   tree

6. "What _____ of a day is this?" asked Frog.

           horse   lot   kind

7. "We _____ to walk!"

        little   love   took

8. "This morning we will _____, said Cat.

                    that   cub   ride

9. "I have a _____ for me and one for you, too!"

          bike   now   went

Name _____

Think about what Joe and Sam liked. Finish the diagram by writing or drawing what each one likes and then what both like.

Joe the Bear likes:

They both like:

Sam the Mouse likes:

☞ Read the directions to children. Guide them through the page or have them finish it independently.

How Joe the Bear and Sam the Mouse Got Together

Name _____

Read each sentence. Write a word from the box to complete each one.

bike	cannot	drum
eat	every	kind
love	ride	place

_____

1. Pig said, "I'm going to _____ on your back, Horse."

_____

2. "What _____ of friend are you?" Horse said.

_____

3. "With you on my back, I _____ run at all."

_____ "

4. "I will have to sit in one _____ .

👉 Read the directions to children. Guide them through the page or have them finish it independently.

Name _____

Write the words that name a special place.

1. I can ride my bike to little lake.

_____

- -

_____

2. I can walk to green park.

_____

- -

_____

3. I can run to fox place.

_____

- -

_____

4. I cannot ride up brown hill!

_____

- -

_____

 Read the directions to children. Guide them through the page or have them finish it independently.

Name _____

A. Next to each word below, write a word from the box to make a compound word. Use the pictures to help you.

box   pen   dog   bird

1. sand _____

2. _____ house

3. _____ house

4. play _____

B. Write a sentence using a compound word.

_____

_____

Read the directions to children. Guide them through the page or have them finish it independently.

HOW JOE THE BEAR AND SAM THE MOUSE GOT TOGETHER

Name _____

Read each sentence and the two words below it. Write a word from the box that stands for the two words.

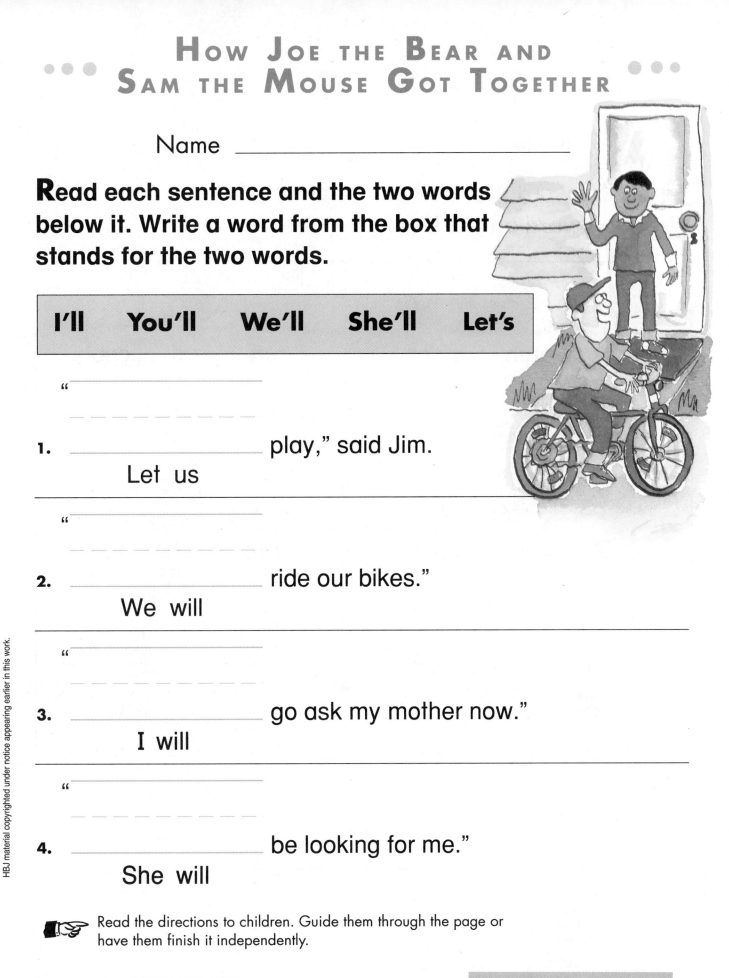

I'll	You'll	We'll	She'll	Let's

" _____

1. _____ play," said Jim.
    Let us

" _____

2. _____ ride our bikes."
    We will

" _____

3. _____ go ask my mother now."
    I will

" _____

4. _____ be looking for me."
    She will

☞ Read the directions to children. Guide them through the page or have them finish it independently.

Name _____

Circle the word that names the picture.
Write the word on the line.

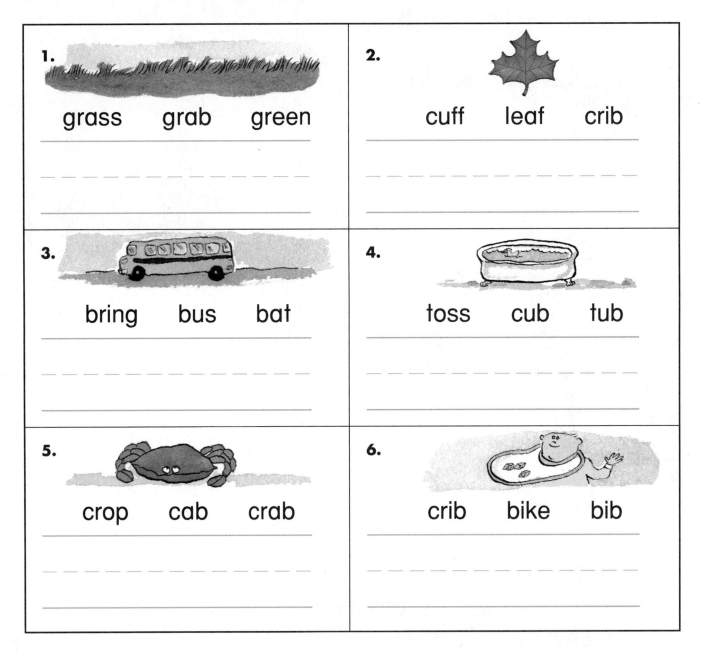

1. grass   grab   green

2. cuff   leaf   crib

3. bring   bus   bat

4. toss   cub   tub

5. crop   cab   crab

6. crib   bike   bib

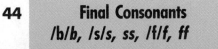 Read the directions to children. Guide them through the page or
have them finish it independently.

Name _____

Look at each picture and read the
sentence. If it could really happen, write
yes. If it could not really happen, write no.

1. Duck can ride a bike. _____

2. Duck can swim. _____

3. Duck can quack. _____

4. Duck says, "Let's go for a swim." _____

5. The baby duck looks for the mother duck. _____

☞ Read the directions to children. Guide them through the page or
have them finish it independently.

Name _____

Read each sentence and the words below it. Write the word that best completes each sentence.

"_____

1. _____, Duck," said Lion.

   Tree   Hello   Could

"_____

2. _____ you like to play?"

   Would   Says   Jump

_____ "

3. Duck said, "Not now, but _____.

   kind   deep   soon

"_____

4. _____ can you play, Duck?" asked Lion.

   You'll   When   Hot

5. "I need to _____ a swim this morning," said Duck.

   take   run   look

☞ Read the directions to children. Guide them through the pages or have them finish independently.

Name _____

6. "Ask the _____ to play," Duck said.
      bike   luck   mouse

_____

_____ "

7. "She is right over _____ .
        there   went   from

_____

8. "Do you see her _____ the house?"
          day   by   this

_____

9. "A mouse is _____ I see," said Lion.
        am   who   very

_____

10. "I wish _____ of you could come and play now."
      swim   bring   both

Name _____

Fill in the story chart.

floor	roots	roof	bugs	birds
ceiling	flowers	cellar	rainbow	

Very Tall Mouse said hello to the:	Very Short Mouse said hello to the:

 Read the directions to children. Guide them through the page or have them finish it independently.

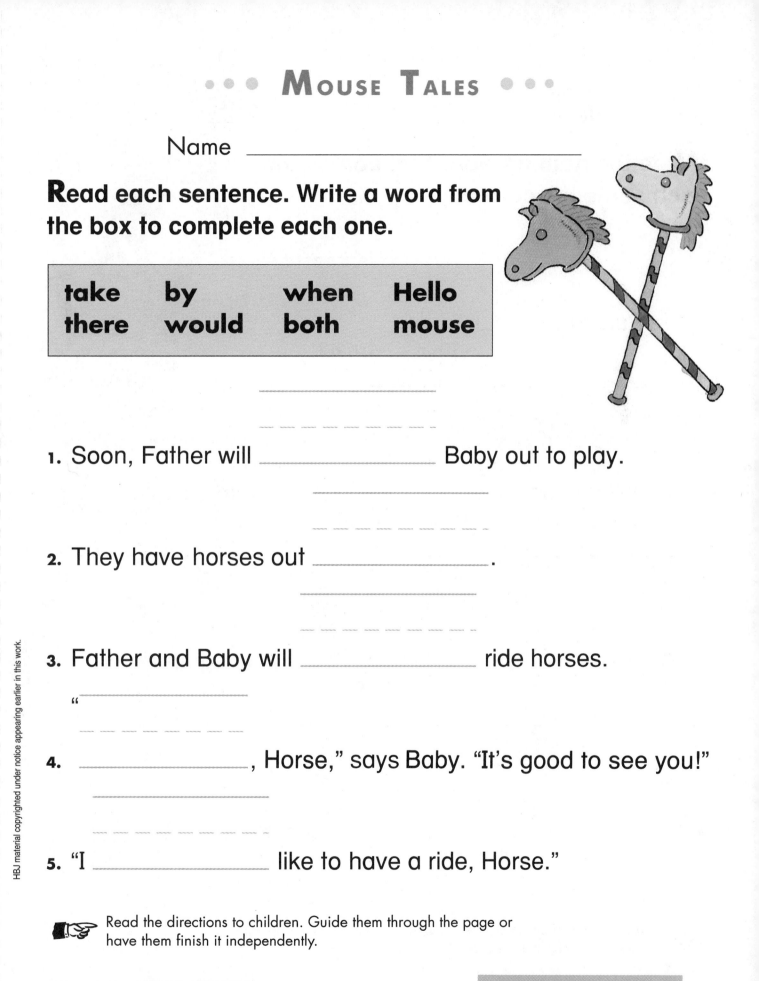

Name _____

Read each sentence. Write a word from the box to complete each one.

take	by	when	Hello
there	would	both	mouse

_____

1. Soon, Father will _____ Baby out to play.

2. They have horses out _____ .

3. Father and Baby will _____ ride horses.

4. "_____ , Horse," says Baby. "It's good to see you!"

5. "I _____ like to have a ride, Horse."

☞ Read the directions to children. Guide them through the page or have them finish it independently.

Name _____

Write the naming word that completes
each sentence correctly.

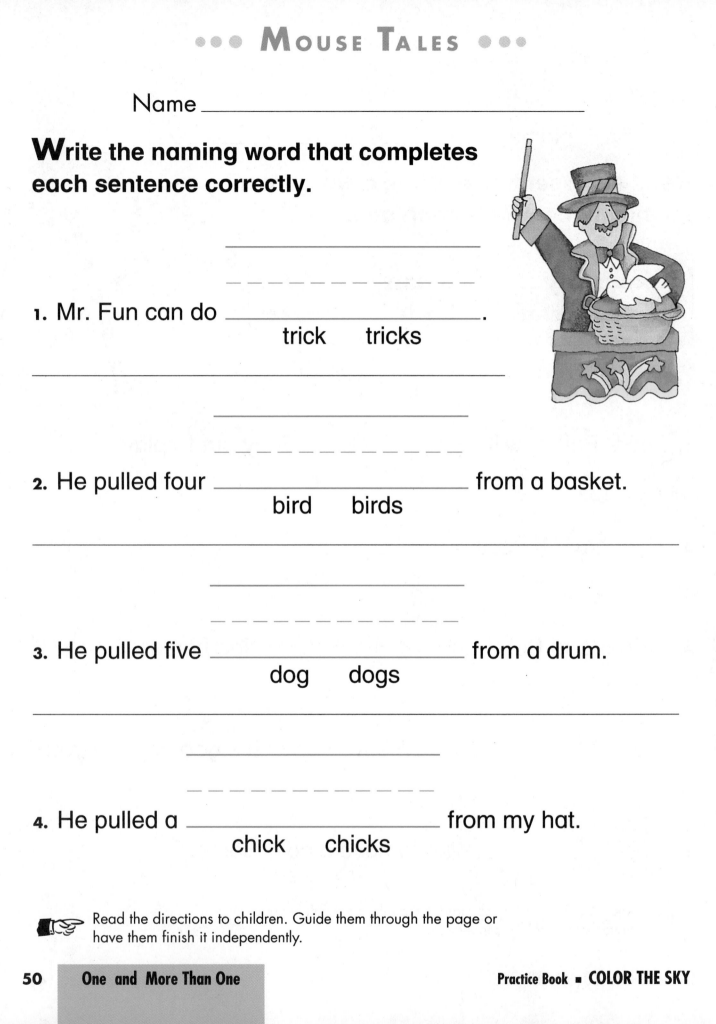

_____
- - - - - - - - - - - -

1. Mr. Fun can do _____ .
    trick   tricks

_____
- - - - - - - - - - - -

2. He pulled four _____ from a basket.
    bird   birds

_____
- - - - - - - - - - - -

3. He pulled five _____ from a drum.
    dog   dogs

_____
- - - - - - - - - - - -

4. He pulled a _____ from my hat.
    chick   chicks

☞ Read the directions to children. Guide them through the page or
  have them finish it independently.

Name _____

Circle the word that names the picture.
Write the word on the line.

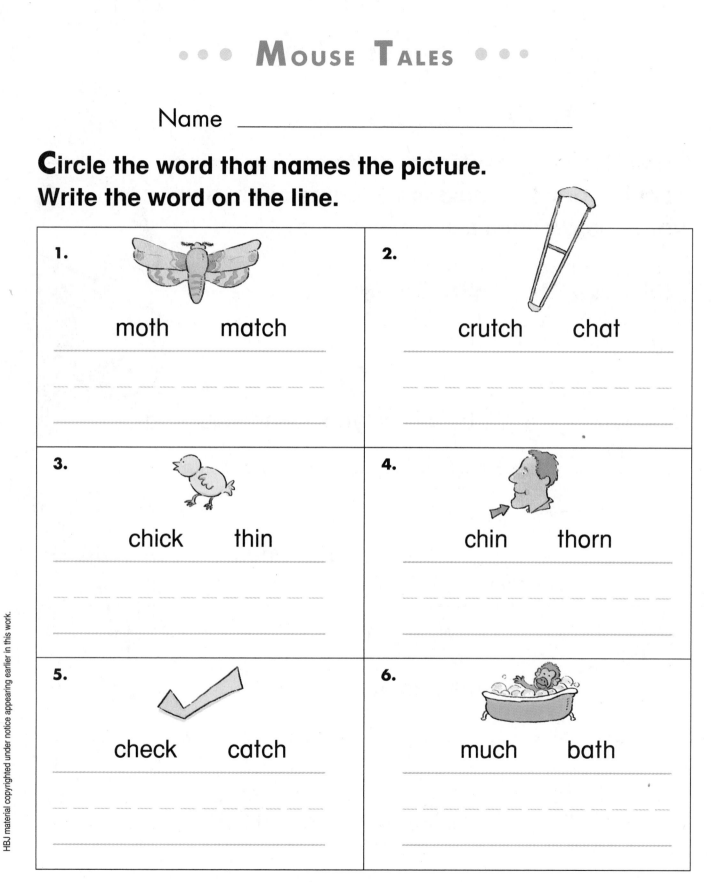

1. moth   match

_____

_____

2. crutch   chat

_____

_____

3. chick   thin

_____

_____

4. chin   thorn

_____

_____

5. check   catch

_____

_____

6. much   bath

_____

_____

☞ Read the directions to children. Guide them through the page or
have them finish it independently.

Name _____

Complete each sentence. Write a contraction from the box that means the same as the two words below each sentence.

I'll   we'll   He'll   Let's

"

1. _____ be seeing you soon," said Tina.
   I will

2. "Then _____ take a bike ride."
   we will

"

3. _____ ask Hal to ride, too."
   Let us

"

4. _____ be happy to see you."
   He will

☞ Read the directions to children. Guide them through the page or have them finish it independently.

Name _____

Look at each picture and read the sentence. If it could really happen, write <u>yes</u>. If it could not really happen, write <u>no</u>.

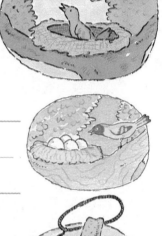

1. The bird will try to fly. _____

2. The bird will soon be a mother bird. _____

3. The bird will catch a horse. _____

4. The bird will make a wish. _____

5. Mother Bird has four baby birds. _____

 Read the directions to children. Guide them through the page or have them finish it independently.

Name _____

**Look at the picture and read each
question. Write the best answer.
Then follow the directions.**

_____

1. Is there a cow? _____

             yes   no

_____

2. How many baby ducks are there? _____

                        one   four   six

_____

3. Who is the mother of the chick? _____

                 the cow   the calf   the hen

_____

4. Make the grass green.

5. Put a tree by the cow.

6. Put a little house where you like.

☞ Read the directions to children. Guide them through the page or
have them finish it independently.